FREEDOM
from
TYRANNY
of the
URGENT

Charles E. Hummel

With Questions for Reflection and Discussion

InterVarsity Press
Downers Grove, Illinois

InterVarsity Press® is the book-publishing division of InterVarsity Christian Fellowship®, a student movement active on campus at hundreds of universities, colleges and schools of nursing in the United States of America, and a member movement of the International Fellowship of Evangelical Students. For information about local and regional activities, write Public Relations Dept., InterVarsity Christian Fellowship, 6400 Schroeder Rd., P.O. Box 7895, Madison, WI 53707-7895.

All Scripture quotations, unless otherwise indicated, are taken from the HOLY BIBLE, NEW INTERNATIONAL VERSION®. NIV®. Copyright ©1973, 1978, 1984 by International Bible Society. Used by permission of Zondervan Publishing House. All rights reserved.

Cover photograph: Andy Whale/Tony Stone Images

ISBN 0-8308-1287-3

Printed in the United States of America ∞

Library of Congress Cataloging-in-Publication Data

Hummel, Charles E.

    Freedom from tyranny of the urgent / Charles E. Hummel.

      p.   cm.

    Includes index.

    ISBN 0-8308-1287-3 (alk. paper)

    1. Time management—Religious aspects—Christianity. I. Title.

BV4598.5.H86   1997

248.4—dc21   97-26150

       ·   CIP

19	18	17	16	15	14	13	12	11	10	9	8	7	6	5	4	3	2	1
13	12	11	10	09	08	07	06	05	04	03	02	01	00	99	98	97		

To Anne

ONE

Where Is Your Time Flying?

Nothing is more characteristic of modern life
than the complaint, "If I only had time."
R. E. NEALE

Have you ever wished for a thirty-hour day? Surely that extra time would relieve the tremendous pressure under which we live. Our lives leave a trail of unfinished tasks. Unanswered letters, unvisited friends, unread books haunt quiet moments when we stop to evaluate what we have accomplished. We desperately need relief.

But would that longer day really solve our problem? Wouldn't we soon be just as frustrated as we are now with our twenty-four-hour allotment?

Nor will the passage of time necessarily help us catch up. Children grow in number and age to require more of our time. Greater experience in profession and church brings demanding assignments. We find ourselves working harder and enjoying life less.

When we stop long enough to think about it, we realize that our dilemma goes deeper than shortage of time; it is basically a problem of priorities. Hard work itself doesn't hurt us. We all know what it is to go full speed for long hours, totally involved in an important task. The resulting weariness is matched by a sense of achievement and joy.

Not hard work, but doubt and misgiving produce anxiety as we review a month or a year and become oppressed by the pile of unfinished tasks. We sense uneasily our failure to do what was really important. The winds of other people's demands, and our own inner compulsions, have driven us onto a reef of frustration. We realize that quite apart from our sins, we have done those things which we ought not to have done, and we have left undone those things which we ought to have done.

An experienced factory manager once said to me, "Your greatest danger is letting the urgent things crowd out the important ones."

> *Our greatest danger is letting the urgent things crowd out the important ones.*

He didn't realize how hard his advice hit. And it applies to every area of life! It has often returned to haunt and rebuke me by raising the critical problem of priorities.

We live in constant tension between the urgent and the important. The problem is that many important tasks need not be done today, or even this week. Additional hours for prayer and Bible study, a visit to an elderly friend, reading an important book: these activities can usually wait a while longer. But often urgent, though less important, tasks call for immediate response and gobble up our time. Endless demands pressure every waking hour.

A person's home is no longer a castle, a private place away from urgent tasks. The telephone breaches its walls with incessant demands. Their appeal seems irresistible, and they devour our energy. But in the light of eternity their momentary prominence fades. With a sense of loss we recall the important tasks that have been shunted aside. We realize that we have become slaves to the tyranny of the urgent.

Timetable Living

Do you ever say, "I just can't fit that into my schedule"? The fast pace of modern life is governed by schedules. With the advent of railroads, buses and airplanes, transportation on a large scale became tied to timetables. The industrial revolution was effected by machines with predictable rates of production. Working hours were adjusted accordingly. Soon private lives, including weekends and vacations, became programmed.

The pressure of attempting to meet these schedules has taken its toll in several areas of life. Later we will trace the history and results of living by the clock. Meanwhile, here we note several significant losses that call for attention.

In the last thirty years the percent of two-income families has more than doubled. As a result, members spend less time together over meals. Breakfast is largely self-serve on different schedules. Dinner often has one or more missing because of late work or school programs, or leaving early for an evening activity. Those who remain at home are often busy with independent projects or sitting in front of the TV or computer.

Even more intriguing and time-consuming for many are the Internet's almost limitless resources. Whatever the schedules of individual activities, they now afford fewer opportunities to strengthen family relationships by spending time together and sharing each other's concerns.

The development of friendships has been both helped and hindered by the car. Although it enables us to visit people more easily and often, we are tempted to schedule several quick calls in one day. The telephone became a boon to keeping in touch, but it has also hastened the demise of correspondence. On the other hand, that lost art has gained a new lease on life on the computer screen through e-mail. (But when you find fifty-seven new messages waiting, you may question whether e-mail is such a blessing . . .)

Full schedule and fast pace have complicated a primary problem in married life: lack of communication. As a husband and wife spend less time with each other, their relationship can become strained by shrinking opportunity for intimacy. Misunderstanding and argument also have a damaging effect on the children.

Another social dimension that suffers is the neighborhood, which frequently becomes little more than a collection of nearby houses. Their inhabitants often have no more time for each other than a wave from the passing car. Although children of the same age usually play with each other, their parents may not spend time with the others from one month to the next. Even with our own friends elsewhere in town, visits become shorter or less frequent.

What accounts for this decline in neighborly relationships? A major reason is that it takes time to be friendly. As a result we tend to avoid helping others in a meaningful way. Like the priest and the Levite in Jesus' parable of the good Samaritan, we tend to pass by on the other side. Or we may not even know when a neighbor needed help until afterward. In situations when we ourselves need personal attention and closer contact with others, the number of people able and willing to provide such assistance is decreasing.

Our lifestyle of full schedule and fast pace also weakens the social fabric of our communities, which depends on a wide range of voluntary groups. In many places organizations such as the local Boy Scouts, Girl Scouts and Red Cross have lost 20 to 25 percent of their membership. At one nearby high school of a thousand students, the once-active Parent Teachers Association has dwindled to half a dozen members despite a variety of different approaches to involve parents. If it doesn't turn around soon, next year will be the last. Within the school participation by students in their own groups is also on the wane.

As Christians we share many of these concerns with others in our community. We place a premium on family values and obligations. Parents want to spend time with their children, to be available to meet their needs, to teach them to love and serve God.

We are also expected to be good neighbors. This responsibility requires time and effort to keep in touch, available to help in case of an emergency. And where called for, to participate in an occasional neighborhood project of mutual concern.

Depending on the civic situation, Christians often feel a responsibility toward the welfare of their community. It may mean volunteering to assist at school, help at the hospital, serve in a soup kitchen or run for the town council.

Furthermore, most of us have church responsibilities. In addition to the main services on Sunday there are church schools and youth fellowships; parish council and committees; Bible studies, prayer-and-praise meetings and special services; evangelistic missions and theological conferences. The pressure of scheduling these activities too often squeezes out time for deepening personal relationships.

> *Are you like the man who jumped on his horse and rode off in all directions?*

How, then, should we deal with the question "Where is your time flying?" The first step is to ask, "Where are *you* flying to catch up? Or running? Or perhaps trudging?" But that presupposes the more basic question, "Where are you *going?* What are your goals in life?"

Position Doubtful!

Perhaps you feel frustrated by not knowing exactly where you are. In 1932 Amelia Earhart became the first woman to fly solo across the Atlantic Ocean. In July 1937, with Frederick Noonan as her navigator, she set out to be the first person to fly around the world at the equator. In the western Pacific near New Guinea she apparently lost her bearings. Her last radio message was "Position doubtful." A massive search by Navy and Coast Guard ships and planes found nothing but ocean.

A fanatic has been described as a person who, when unsure of his direction, doubles his speed. Have you recently been traveling faster than usual? While you are probably not a fanatic, your fast pace may be an indication that you have lost your sense of direction.

If so, isn't this is a good time to slow down and take your bearings?

The following pages are designed to meet the need for a short book that is biblical and practical. Neither exhaustive nor exhausting, it is for readers who have little time to read about time. These chapters point a way for you to get beyond the tyranny of the urgent and enjoy the freedom offered by our Lord Jesus Christ to those who love and serve him.

* * *

Questions for Reflection and Discussion

1. What unfinished tasks are of greatest concern to you right now?

2. What urgent demands of others weigh most heavily on you?

3. List the two or three most important goals in your life for the next six months to a year.

4. When did you last take at least a full hour to check your direction and take your bearings?

5. At this point, what time slot each week could you reserve to start reviewing your activities and reshaping your priorities and schedule?

TWO

Jesus
& Time

Father, the time has come . . .
I have brought you glory on earth
by completing the work you gave me to do.
JESUS

*A*mong the ancient Middle Eastern nations Israel stood alone
in its linear view of history. God's people remembered their past—
their founding as a nation through Abraham and their deliverance
from Egypt through Moses. They also looked forward to a time
when the Messiah would come to establish his universal kingdom.
For Israel, history was on the move toward a glorious goal.

The apostle Paul writes, "When the time had fully come, God
sent his Son" (Gal 4:4). After nearly four centuries of prophetic
silence, the angel Gabriel suddenly appeared to announce the
coming of Christ. "He will be great and will be called the Son of
the Most High. The Lord God will give him the throne of his father
David . . . his kingdom will never end" (Lk 1:32-33).

Not only Israel but also the secular world had been prepared by
God for this event. The Roman Empire provided political stability
and an excellent transportation system. The Greek language was

spoken and read throughout much of the empire. This unique situation was ideal for the spread of the Christian message. The time was right.

The Kingdom of God

Around the age of thirty, Jesus came to John the Baptist to be baptized. Then he went into the desert for forty days of temptation. Upon his return to Galilee he preached and healed in the power of the Spirit. " 'The time [kairos] has come,' he said. 'The kingdom of God is near. Repent and believe the good news!' " (Mk 1:15).

Jesus' coming climaxed centuries of waiting. The Hebrews had long recognized God as not only the Creator and Sustainer of the universe but also the Lord and Judge of history. The idea of his universal kingship pervades the Old Testament. For example, "The LORD your God is God in heaven above and on the earth below" (Josh 2:11). God's people looked forward with longing to the time when his governance would be universally recognized. "The LORD will be king over the whole earth. On that day there will be one LORD, and his name the only name" (Zech 14:9).

In Jesus of Nazareth the kingdom has arrived. It is evidenced by his authoritative preaching, teaching and healing. His power over the forces of Satan and his other miracles are signs of the kingdom. Its blessings—forgiveness and eternal life—are available to us in our present moment.

This kingdom is not just a spiritual realm high above the concerns of human history. Nor is it a matter of geography and national boundaries. *It is God's gracious rule in the hearts and lives of his people.* Jesus and his apostles announce the present reality of the kingdom of God amid daily life. On one occasion Jesus declares, "The kingdom of God is within [or among] you" (Lk 17:21).

Nevertheless, Jesus makes it clear that the full realization of the kingdom of God is future. Meanwhile we are instructed to be active: "But seek first his kingdom and his righteousness, and all these things will be given to you as well" (Mt 6:33). Sacrifice to gain the

kingdom is worthwhile (Mt 13:44-45). Yet it is a gift of God that
he will fulfill in his own time (Mt 25:34).

The Lord's Prayer opens with these words:

Our Father in heaven,

hallowed be your name,

your kingdom come,

your will be done

on earth as it is in heaven. (Mt 6:9-10)

Jesus equates the presence of the kingdom with doing the will of
God. In the following chapters we will see the significance of the
kingdom of God—and the importance of living as kingdom people—as we set personal goals and utilize our time to reach them.
Meanwhile, we will consider Jesus' use of time in his three years
of ministry.

Finding the Right Time

What was Jesus' mission and how did he go about fulfilling it? He
summed up his activities in a brief statement: "For even the Son of
Man did not come to be served, but to serve, and to give his life as
a ransom for many" (Mk 10:45). A life of service and a death of
sacrifice.

According to the Gospel of John, Jesus fulfills this purpose by
doing his Father's works and speaking his Father's words. Time
and again he affirms this reality: "The words I say to you are not
just my own. Rather, it is the Father, living in me, who is doing his
work" (Jn 14:10; see also 4:34; 5:19, 30, 36; 6:38; 8:38; 14:24, 31;
15:15; 17:4, 8).

Jesus carries out this mission through the guidance and power
of the Holy Spirit (Lk 4:1, 14). At the outset of his ministry, in his
hometown of Nazareth, he claims in a synagogue sermon the
fulfillment of Isaiah's prophecy:

The Spirit of the Lord is on me,

because he has anointed me

to preach good news to the poor.

He has sent me to proclaim freedom for the prisoners
  and recovery of sight for the blind,
to release the oppressed,
  to proclaim the year of the Lord's favor. (Lk 4:18-19)
Prominent in Jesus' ministry is not only a resolve to make good use
of his short length of time but also a sense of *the right time for action.*

Sometimes a bad guess, or a wrong motive, or just plain laziness,
may throw our timing off. We get tired of holding the announced
Bible study each week because no one is showing up. So we
quit—and the following week three people come by, only to find
they are too late. Or we fire off a heated reply to a controversial
letter before we stop to pray and to look at the situation from all
angles—and our reply, instead of solving things, just adds fuel to
the fire.

Things done at the wrong time may turn out to be not worth doing
at all—simply a waste of time—or even harmful.

The Gospel of John records nine occurrences of the concept of
timing; twice it is expressed by *kairos* ("opportune time"), and
seven times by the word *hōra* ("hour"). The latter is often used
figuratively to indicate the arrival of a crucial or opportune time.
We see these elements in two remarkable situations in Jesus'
ministry that offer a good example for us in our activities.

A Change of Plans
Both Mark (1:21-39) and Luke (4:31-44) record a very busy day
near the beginning of Jesus' ministry. His activities reveal commitment to his mission coupled with sensitivity to a leading of the
Spirit that takes a surprising turn.

Jesus' prophetic preaching in Nazareth infuriates the people.
They drive him out of town and attempt to throw him over a cliff.
But he escapes and goes on to Capernaum, a town in Galilee. There,
on a sabbath in the synagogue, Jesus begins to teach the people.
They are amazed because, unlike their teachers of the law, he speaks
with authority.

Suddenly the service is interrupted with the cries of a man possessed by an evil spirit. When Jesus commands him to be quiet and come out, the demon leaves the man with a shriek. The people are even more amazed by Jesus' power to cast out evil spirits. The news quickly spreads throughout the whole region of Galilee.

Upon leaving the synagogue Jesus goes to the home of Andrew and Simon, where Simon's mother-in-law is in bed with a high fever. What an embarrassing turn of events for the hostess! When Jesus is asked to help her, he rebukes the fever, and it leaves her. She immediately gets up and begins to wait on the guests.

As the sun is setting to end the sabbath, the people bring to the door all who have various kinds of sickness and demon possession. Jesus lays his hands on each one and heals them. Even though the evil spirits know that he is the Messiah, Jesus will not let them speak.

After such a demanding day and night, surely Jesus deserves to have a long sleep. Yet Mark tells us, "Very early in the morning, while it was still dark, Jesus got up, left the house and went off to a solitary place, where he prayed" (1:35). While we are not told the content of his prayer, we can surmise from what happens afterward that it included asking for guidance for the day ahead.

Soon those who were not healed the night before begin to gather outside the house. As time goes on and Jesus does not appear, the crowd grows restless. Imagine their bewilderment and concern. And think of the embarrassment of the disciples and Peter's mother-in-law, who are forced to admit that they don't know where the honored guest has gone.

So Simon and his companions go to look for Jesus. When they find their leader they exclaim, "Everyone is looking for you!" We can hear the tone of exasperation and reproach. Meanwhile the people, who are also looking for Jesus, come to where he is and try to keep him from leaving. But he answers, "I must preach the good news of the kingdom of God to the other towns also, because that is why I was sent" (Lk 4:43). So, surrounded by urgent opportunities for ministry right where he is, Jesus uses the morning to begin a trip to another town, preaching in the synagogue and driving out demons.

We might have said, "Seize the moment, Jesus! Show your power; win people to God!"

And Jesus would have answered us, "Early this morning the Father showed me today's priorities."

Although we are not told the reactions of the people left behind, we can easily imagine a range of emotions from surprise and disappointment to anger and despair. Put yourself in the place of Peter's mother-in-law, the people who are still not healed, the disciples who have left all to follow Jesus. How would you feel as Jesus turns and walks away?

> *"I have come down from heaven not to do my will but to do the will of him who sent me."*

Or put yourself in the place of Jesus himself. How must he feel leaving behind such sorrow as well as joy? The choice between two important tasks is most painful: a yes to one of them is a no to the other. Jesus' decision to preach and heal in another town that day means leaving behind people who are still in great need. Yet Jesus is letting the Father set his schedule.

Here, at the outset of Mark's Gospel, we find the secret of Jesus' ministry. He was not given a divinely drawn blueprint or advance schedule. Day by day he prayerfully listened for the Father's instructions. Luke emphasizes the role of the Holy Spirit. After his baptism by John, Jesus was led by the Spirit in the wilderness. After his extended temptation, Jesus returned to Galilee where he was empowered by the Spirit to discern and to perform the will of the Father.

In that way Jesus was able to resist urgent—even legitimate, at times desperate—demands in order to do what was really important, the will of the Father. It meant taking his life and work step by step.

We too need to listen so that we can follow. In chapter eight we will talk about finding spiritual refreshment and direction by taking time out with God.

"You Weren't Here in Time!"

In his itinerant ministry, Jesus faced great human need. He put in long hours, ate irregular meals and slept in a different place every few nights. "Foxes have holes and birds of the air have nests, but the Son of Man has no place to lay his head" (Mt 8:20).

With no home of his own, Jesus was warmly welcomed in the village of Bethany, not far from Jerusalem. He always had a place in the hearts and home of sisters Martha and Mary and their brother Lazarus. It was there, at a dinner given in Jesus' honor six days before the Passover, that Mary poured perfume on his feet and wiped them with her hair (Jn 12:3).

In the next scene, far from Bethany, Jesus is engaged in a fruitful ministry. One day the sisters send an urgent message: "Lord, the one you love is sick" (Jn 11:3). When he hears the news, Jesus gives an encouraging reply. He declares that this sickness will not end in death; rather it is for the glory of God and his Son. The Gospel writer then makes a perplexing and seemingly contradictory statement: "Jesus loved Martha and her sister and Lazarus. Yet when he heard that Lazarus was sick, he stayed where he was two more days" (vv. 5-6).

Our immediate reaction is "What kind of love is that?" How would you like to be in the shoes of the messenger who has to carry that decision back to the distraught sisters? Imagine the reaction of those faithful friends, now caught in a life-and-death struggle as their brother grows weaker, yet with no further word from their Lord.

Two days after receiving the message Jesus says to his disciples, "Let us go back to Judea. . . . Lazarus is dead, and for your sake I am glad I was not there, so that you may believe. But let us go to him" (vv. 7, 15).

When they arrive, Lazarus has been in the tomb four days; family and friends are on hand to comfort the sisters. Martha hears that Jesus is coming and goes to meet him outside the village. There she greets him with a mixture of reproach and faith: "Lord . . . if you had been here, my brother would not have died. But I know that even now God will give you whatever you ask" (vv. 21-22). Jesus replies, "Your brother will rise again. . . . I am the resurrection and the life. He who believes in me will live, even though he dies" (vv. 23, 25).

Martha then goes back to the house, calls Mary aside and says, "The Teacher is here . . . and is asking for you" (v. 28). Followed by the mourners, Mary quickly goes out to the place where Jesus is. She falls at his feet, and she too says, "Lord, if you had been here, my brother would not have died" (v. 32).

When he sees everyone weeping, Jesus is deeply moved and troubled. As they walk toward the tomb he also weeps. The friends are impressed with how deeply he loves Lazarus. Some of them wonder whether he who opened the eyes of the blind could also have kept Lazarus from dying.

When they come to the tomb—a cave with a stone laid across the entrance—Jesus commands that the stone be taken away. He then calls with a loud voice, "Lazarus, come out!" (v. 43). The dead man comes out, his hands and feet still wrapped with strips of linen and a cloth still covering his face. Jesus says to them, "Take off the grave clothes and let him go" (v. 44).

In this account the sisters' *urgent* need was to prevent the death of their beloved brother. But the *important* thing from God's point of view was to raise Lazarus from the dead. So he was allowed to die, and his sisters were allowed to grieve. As a result the resurrection of Lazarus is a powerful sign of Jesus' claim "I am the resurrection and the life" and of his promise of life to those who believe in him. Those words have comforted countless Christians in every generation at the deaths of those whom they love.

Jesus did get there at the right time, after all.

The Father's Work

We now come to the Passover feast in Jerusalem. Jesus knows that he has come to the end of his earthly ministry. After four chapters of upper-room instruction for his disciples, he prays for himself.

Father, the time has come. Glorify your Son, that your Son may glorify you. For you granted him authority over all people that he might give eternal life to all those you have given him. . . . I have brought you glory on earth by completing the work you gave me to do. (Jn 17:1-2, 4)

How could Jesus talk about a "completed" work? His three-year ministry seems painfully brief. One prostitute at a banquet was given forgiveness and a new life, but many others still ply their trade. For every withered muscle that flexed into strength, hundreds remain crippled. The blind, maimed and diseased abound throughout the country. Yet on that last night, with many urgent human needs unmet and useful tasks undone, the Lord has peace.

The answer to our question lies in one word: "the work *you* gave me to do." Jesus did not meet all the human needs he encountered—many urgently desired by family and friends, and by others along his path. But he completed the mission *his Father* gave him.

In *The Discipline and Culture of the Spiritual Life,* A. E. Whiteham observes:

Here in this Man is adequate purpose . . . inward rest that gives an air of leisure to his crowded life. Above all there is in this Man a secret and a power of dealing with the waste-products of life: pain, disappointment, enmity, death. He made a short life of about thirty years, abruptly cut off, to be a "finished" life. We cannot admire the poise and beauty of this human life and then ignore the things that made it.

In the following chapters we will see how this principle exemplified by our Lord can free us from the tyranny of the urgent in our own Christian life and work.

* * *

Questions for Reflection and Discussion

1. How does the Holy Spirit play a key role in the opening events of this chapter?

2. What aspect of the kingdom of God is most meaningful to you at present?

3. With whom do you most identify in the events at Capernaum?

4. Have you ever been in the position of Martha and Mary as they sent an urgent request to Jesus and received no answer?

THREE

Managing
Your Life

The yield of our life does not depend so much
on the number of things that we do,
but more on the quality of the self-giving
we put into each thing.
PAUL TOURNIER

*O*ne day in the 1920s Charles Schwab, president of Bethlehem Steel, met Ivy Lee, pioneer management consultant. The industrial magnate said, "Show me a way to get more things done with my time, and I'll pay you anything within reason."

Lee handed him a blank sheet of paper and told him to take a few minutes that evening to write down in order of priority the six most important tasks he had to do. The next day he was to work on item number one until he had finished it, then pass on to item two, and so on down the list. At the end of the day he should tear up the list and make a new one for the following day.

"Don't be concerned," Lee advised, "if you finish only one or two tasks. Your main objective is not necessarily to do them all, but to spend your time on those that are the most important. In other words, *do first things first.* If you can't finish all the tasks on the list by this method, you couldn't by any other method, either. And without some system, you'd probably not even have decided which were the most important. When you have tried this method, send me a check for what you think it's worth."

A few weeks later Schwab mailed Lee a check for $25,000 (equivalent to about ten times that much today), with a note saying that it was the most profitable lesson he had ever learned.

Ivy Lee's procedure sets daily priorities among a list of current tasks calling for action. But it doesn't begin to deal with the more basic question of what items are simply urgent at the moment and not really important for the long run. How do the tasks scheduled for today, even those near the top of the list, contribute to our goals?

In this chapter we will focus on square one—goals and values of the kingdom of God under the lordship of Jesus Christ. In the following chapters we will explain how to manage our activities with the use of four basic steps.

Kingdom Goals

As Christians we have been brought into the kingdom of God, his gracious rule in our lives. The apostle Paul tells us that since we are a new creation in Christ, the old has passed away; everything has become new. "From now on, therefore, we regard no one from a human point of view" (2 Cor 5:16 NRSV). We have a new perspective on life under the management of our Lord in the power of the Holy Spirit.

The New Testament explains what this means for the way we use our time.

Be careful then how you live, not as unwise people but as wise, making the most of [redeeming] the time [opportunity], because the days are evil. (Eph 5:15-16 NRSV)

Conduct yourselves wisely toward outsiders, making the most of the time [opportunity]. (Col 4:5 NRSV)

But encourage one another daily, as long as it is called Today, so that none of you may be hardened by sin's deceitfulness. (Heb 3:13)

Some Christians conclude from these commands that God requires "busyness" in his service. Not to be "busy" is considered a lack of commitment and good stewardship, so days, evenings and weekends are filled with church meetings and other activities. The context of these verses, however, reveals a different meaning.

The first two verses call not for hard work but for wise conduct toward outsiders. The word translated "making the most of the time" is better rendered by the term "redeeming." We are called to "deliver" or "free" our time from unimportant activities. The word for time here is *kairos* ("opportunity"). The emphasis is not on *duration*—the passing hours and minutes of our day, but on *timeliness*—a ripe time for extending the kingdom of God. Yet how can we do this in an already overloaded schedule?

We need to reevaluate our priorities and free up some time to make the most of important opportunities. We'll talk more about priorities in chapter four.

The third verse above, regarding exhortation, also emphasizes making use of opportunities while they are present. "Today" is the day of divine grace and opportunity to serve God, so make good use of the present time while it is available for you to warn and encourage one another.

Our goal is to discover God's will for us day by day at each stage of life. There is no substitute for the confidence that today—in this time and place—I am obeying the will of my Father. Such guidance and inner peace is the work of the Holy Spirit in the lives of Christians. He interprets and applies the Word of God to our present situation as he guides our planning.

> *There is no substitute for the confidence that today—in this time and place—I am obeying the will of my Father.*

In his parables our Lord often pictures life as stewardship. He tells stories of good and bad stewards, according to the way they manage their masters' affairs. Jesus says, "From everyone to whom much has been given, much will be required" (Lk 12:48 NRSV). Paul

writes, "It is required of stewards that they be found trustworthy"
(1 Cor 4:2 NRSV). And Peter instructs, "Like good stewards of the
manifold grace of God, serve one another with whatever gift each
of you has received" (1 Pet 4:10 NRSV).

Becoming Free

Yet a nagging question remains. We are told to look at life from
God's point of view, live carefully, make the most of our opportunities and be good stewards of our talents. But how is this possible
amid the many pressures we face? It is one thing to recognize the
tyranny of the urgent in our lives, but another to discover a way of
becoming free from its grip.

We have seen the example of Jesus doing the Father's will, but
where is the power for us to follow it? Good resolutions to reorganize our life wear thin. We must turn to the promise of the Lord
himself for a solution to this problem.

One day at the temple in Jerusalem, Jesus challenges the Jewish
leaders with his claim to be the light of the world. He says that his
teaching comes from God. Jesus declares, "I tell you the truth,
everyone who sins is a slave to sin. . . . So if the Son sets you free,
you will be free indeed" (Jn 8:34, 36). His hearers react violently,
claiming that they have never been slaves to anyone. They seem
oblivious to the political as well as spiritual slavery that fetters them
at that moment.

Obviously there was disagreement over the meaning of freedom
then as there is today. In popular use it means simply absence of
hindrance, confinement, repression. However, that meaning is
negative; it defines what freedom is *not*. But why should we want
to be free? Only when we get beyond freedom *from* restraint and
ask about freedom *for* a purpose can we understand its true meaning. Only then will we understand the basic elements of limitation
and responsibility inherent in the nature of freedom itself.

Freedom is a condition in which something can fulfill the pur-
pose for which it is designed. This principle is evident in everyday

life. For example, an automobile is designed to run swiftly on a paved road. Yet it is free to do so only as long as it stays on the road. If it seeks greater "freedom" by suddenly turning off into the bushes, the vehicle comes to a grinding halt, possibly injuring or killing its passengers.

We can understand the meaning of human freedom only when we know the purpose for which we were designed. What are we set free *for?* The Bible portrays humankind created in the image of God for a life of loving obedience to our Creator. We are free to obey God; free to express his love to those around us; free to take care of the earth and its creatures.

But according to both the Old and New Testaments, something has gone radically wrong. Taking our destiny into our own hands, we have turned off the road of God's will into the ditch of self-determination. We have violated God's rules—and crashed. The results appear on the front page of the daily paper, on the TV news and in the fractured relationships all around us.

Jesus Christ came to deal with the problem of sin—its penalty and power. That is why he told the people of Jerusalem that he was able to free them from the slavery of sin.

Jesus had a further word for those who believed in him: "If you continue in my word, you are truly my disciples; and you will know the truth, and the truth will make you free" (Jn 8:31-32 NRSV).

Here Jesus is not talking about the simple acquisition of knowledge. Wrenched from its context, the motto "The truth will make you free" is chiseled in marble over library doors on dozens of campuses across the country. The idea that our basic human problem is ignorance is a prevalent myth. Yet knowledge itself liberates no one; our chief enemy is not ignorance but sin. C. S. Lewis noted that higher education often enables people to become more clever devils.

The apostle Paul has a more realistic view of life. He candidly admits, "I have the desire to do what is good, but I cannot carry it out" (Rom 7:18). He shares his agonizing struggle against an inner evil compulsion to sin. He cries out, "Who will rescue me?" The answer: "Jesus Christ our Lord" (vv. 24-25).

Jesus teaches his followers an essential of discipleship: "If you continue in my word." It means a life of commitment to his teaching, acting on what we already know. In that context we keep on learning the truth about God, ourselves and others, about his purpose for our life and the problems we face. In the process our Lord also frees us from the tyranny of the urgent in our daily lives.

St. Augustine expressed a paradox of the Christian life: "Slavery to God is perfect freedom." In other words, commitment to the will of God—the purpose for which we are designed—offers freedom to become the person we are meant to be—freedom to travel along the road of God's choice.

"Time Management"

Early in the twentieth century, management sciences developed time-and-motion studies to evaluate workers' activities and increase their productivity. Slow-motion cameras and calculators were used to analyze jobs and eliminate unnecessary labor.

Eventually time-management principles and techniques for manufacturing were applied upward from the assembly line to the company president. This approach also spread to the public sector and to professional, religious and charitable organizations. In recent decades a wave of books and seminars has inundated the market to deal with the unrelenting pressures of modern life.

Belatedly many churches caught up with the secular world in the use of management principles. Christian advocates of this approach, who had begun their management careers in business and industry, were appalled to discover large numbers of poorly administered churches, mission societies and schools. Soon seminars and books by evangelicals equaled the quality of those in the secular world.

Time-management tools have produced better stewardship of personnel and financial resources. These tools can be effective for the church's future as long as they serve goals of the kingdom of God.

Yet we need to recognize that the term "time management" is a misnomer. A person cannot do anything to time itself—delay or hasten, save or lose it—much less "manage" it. The challenge is to manage *ourselves* under the lordship of Jesus Christ, from whom we get our goals and values. The basic question is what we do *within* the time frame granted to us—how we plan, decide, organize, evaluate, revise our tasks. The bottom line is *managing ourselves within the time frame granted to us.* This is what we really mean when we use the popular misnomer "time management."

> *The challenge is to manage ourselves under the lordship of Jesus Christ, from whom we get our goals and values.*

In the following chapters we will explore a method that puts these principles into practice. The four basic steps are

1. Set priorities (chapter four).
2. Take inventory (chapter five).
3. Budget the hours (chapter six).
4. Implement the plan (chapter seven).

This method isn't a formula for success—one, two, three, four and the bell rings. Although the four steps follow a logical order, they can run concurrently. Some are used more frequently; all are needed along the path of more productive use of our abilities and energy, free from tyranny of the urgent under the lordship of Christ.

* * *

Questions for Reflection and Discussion

1. How do you respond to Ivy Lee's method of determining the priorities of a day's activities?

2. In what way has your new life in Christ changed your outlook in an important area of life?

3. What do you think about the definition of freedom in this chapter? How might it be relevant to your situation?

4. In what way do you feel the Holy Spirit is guiding you to discern and do the will of God?

5. What are some barriers you find in trying to manage yourself?

FOUR

Is This
Trip Necessary?

*Put first things first
and we get second things thrown in;
put second things first
and we lose both first and second things.*
C. S. LEWIS

*R*ecently the president of a prestigious university was asked
to meet with a key faculty committee. Its members were struggling
with proposed budget items covering academic programs for the
coming year. They had just read a report on the growing endowment
fund, now almost half a billion dollars. In that light the faculty
request for increased funding in several significant departments
seemed reasonable.

The president sketched for the committee the university's
overall financial picture, with important new budget requirements in other areas. He said, "No matter how large an institu-
tion's resources, priorities must be set and hard decisions must
be made."

Before we see how this principle applies on the personal level,
let's look back at attempts to solve the problem of limited resources
mainly by achieving greater productivity.

How Efficient Can We Be?

The watchword of the industrial revolution was *efficiency.* Machinery for chemical and mechanical processes was constantly redesigned for higher production at lower costs. This goal steadily infiltrated other areas of life—including the home, for which "labor-saving" devices were invented and promoted.

Efficiency also became the watchword of the early time-management movement with its time-and-motion studies of organizational personnel and procedures. Their goal was promoted with the slogan "Work smarter, not harder." The promised reward? Well-managed job time leaves evenings, weekends and holidays free for other activities. There should be ample time for family, leisure, community and civic involvement. Time-management methods, suitably modified, will increase efficiency in running the home, organizing a vacation, even nurturing our devotional life. Behold the millennium, with lions and lambs the best of friends!

Yet that promise has not been fulfilled. We wonder why the dream never came true. One reason is the Law of Unintended Consequences: unforeseen negative byproducts that undermine the planned benefits. For example, a labor-saving device like the computer increases the range of possible programs, but it often devours more time and produces larger quantities of paper than previously. For busy executives the relative ease and low expense of e-mail is proving to be an unexpected burden. Each morning the computer greets them with a large collection of messages that call for evaluation and urgent action. The added burden can spark nostalgia for the former "in" basket stack of letters!

> *"Work expands to fill the time available."*
> *—Parkinson*

Another reason for the failed promises of management consultants is Parkinson's Principle: *Work expands to fill the time available.* This tendency, which Parkinson observed in government bureaucracies, also applies to the lives of individuals. Even substantial improvements in efficiency do not automatically save the expected amount of time. Somehow the organization or individual spends it on other activities whose urgency makes them seem important.

Effective Living

How is it that hard work and greater efficiency do not necessarily result in a sense of achievement? The answer has been given by an influential pioneer and promoter of management principles and practice.

Peter Drucker realized that efficiency experts were barking up the wrong tree. He drew a crucial distinction between two words often used as synonyms: *efficient* and *effective*. For example, a dictionary defines *efficient* as "acting or producing effectively with a minimum of waste, expense or unnecessary effort." But *effective* is defined as "having an intended or expected effect." Between the two words there can be a world of difference. *Efficient* emphasizes the means of production, the degree of economy with which it is carried out. On the other hand, *effective* focuses on the result or purpose for which the activity is carried out.

In wartime the armed forces have top priority for use of the nation's resources. In World War II, facilities for manufacturing automobiles were converted to producing various kinds of military vehicles—from Jeeps to armored personnel carriers and tanks. Gasoline for civilians was tightly rationed. Yet there were extra allocations for special needs of the war effort; for example, a person driving to and from a defense job would receive extra gasoline coupons.

People were urged to make more efficient use of their cars by driving slowly and doubling up whenever possible. At the same time, across the country prominent posters urged everyone to ask the most important question: "Is this trip necessary?"

Drucker noted that by using a minimum amount of energy and time, we can be very *efficient* in performing a certain task. Yet our work is actually *effective* only when it contributes to our goals. *True effectiveness is not a matter of doing things right but of doing the right things.* For example, you may work out a very efficient, detailed procedure for keeping personal financial records. But before you congratulate yourself you should ask the basic question: Are those records necessary?

The effective person doesn't let the apparent success of being more efficient mask the mistake of performing an activity that is not important. The crucial question is not short-term efficiency but rather long-term effectiveness. In other words, how significant is the task at hand?

Step One: Set Priorities

Our procedure for setting priorities is based on the important/urgent model which we looked at earlier. Here every task is evaluated by its degree of being important and/or urgent. Activities range across the entire spectrum; some are completely at one extreme or the other, but most tasks lie somewhere in the middle.

Importance is gauged by contribution to our high priority goals. Important tasks that are not urgent require initiative and perseverance. Since frequently there is no pressure for them to be done today, this week or even this month, these activities must be motivated by our commitment to their ultimate value. Examples are long-range planning, relationship-building, recreation.

Urgency calls for immediate attention. Urgent matters come into our life demanding action. Often the initiative is taken by someone else; the tasks are of most value to that person. They are more an interruption than a contribution to our own priorities. Examples are a telephone call, fax message, e-mail, knock on the door.

Most of our activities are marked by a tension—often a contest—between these two factors: importance and urgency. Following are various combinations which can help us evaluate proposed tasks.

Important—Urgent. These activities obviously have the highest current priority because they deal with significant results and require immediate action. Although not on the schedule, they elbow their way to the top of the list. Examples are an unexpected major problem, crisis, impending deadline.

Important—Not Urgent. These activities have high priority even though they do not require immediate action. Examples are planning, revision of goals, strengthening relationships. Although at the heart of effective personal management, these activities are often neglected because they do not have to be done now. They become costly casualties of tyranny of the urgent.

Not Important—Urgent. Although unimportant, these activities in the guise of urgency conjure up an illusion that they are of value to us. They include interruptions of many kinds: some phone calls, meetings, visitors, requests for information. They can keep us busy for hours meeting other people's expectations.

With the aid of these categories you can identify the priorities of your activities. When you say, "I don't have time for this task," you really mean, "I don't consider it as important as something else I want or need to do." For whatever reason, you have decided to use the hours another way. The issue is not lack of time but a choice you have made.

The first step is to decide what activities are most important so that you can plan to give them the proper priority during the course of a day, week or month. The key is not to prioritize the activities on your schedule, but to schedule your predetermined priorities.

You may wish to list your "top ten" activities in order of, first, importance and, second, urgency. Then see how well the two lists match, and make a third list that considers both urgency and importance. Finally, follow that list, carrying out the tasks strictly in the order listed. (See figure 1.)

There is no blueprint for all Christians in the use of their time, any more than there is for spending their money. God has given us widely differing abilities, amounts of energy, opportunities, responsibilities and personal needs. In that light, instead of comparing

TOP TEN IMPORTANT TASKS	TOP TEN URGENT TASKS	ORDER IN WHICH TASKS WILL BE DONE
1.	1.	1.
2.	2.	2.
3.	3.	3.
4.	4.	4.
5.	5.	5.
6.	6.	6.
7.	7.	7.
8.	8.	8.
9	9.	9.
10.	10.	10.
		11.
		12.
		13.
		14.
		15.
		16.
		17.
		18.
		19.
		20.

Figure 1.   Identifying Priorities.   Photocopying privileges granted.

yourself to someone else, realistically consider the basic components of what for you is a productive Christian life. Ask God, "What are your priorities for my life right now?" You can then prayerfully set appropriate personal goals.

At this point your job and its components should not be included. That area of activity warrants separate treatment. Here your activities will include the dimension of personal relationships—with God, family, neighbors, friends. Ask yourself, *Who are the important people in my life, and what claim do they have on my time?* In addition, are there community duties and programs (school, neighborhood, church)? And don't forget about personal needs such as hobbies, recreation, exercise, solitude.

As you review the major areas of your life, select four or five important activities that you feel are being neglected or need improvement. Write down a "goal for growth" for each one and indicate the frequency: how many times per day, week, month or year. (See figure 2.)

For example, devotions may be daily; an exercise program may call for four sessions a week. Church activities of worship and service are usually weekly. Other projects may be monthly; an annual vacation will be an oasis once a year (guard it carefully!). Listing these estimated periods will be helpful when you plan a schedule in chapter seven.

Keep in mind that this is a preliminary draft, a trial run. It will give you practice in using the simple four-step procedure. Many time-management seminars feature lengthy, complicated programs in thick notebooks and manuals. Yet back home, amid the pressures of life, they are often put aside on a shelf to rest in peace, pending more time to put them to use.

Reflect on the relative importance of the goals you have selected, but do not start making a schedule yet. So far you have simply identified some of the most valuable activities in your life. Before you can plan the time of future activities you need to look at patterns of the past.

IMPORTANT ACTIVITY OR RELATIONSHIP THAT NEEDS HIGHER PRIORITY	ACTION I WILL TAKE	FREQUENCY
1.		
2.		
3.		
4.		
5.		

Figure 2.   Goals for Growth.   Photocopying privileges granted.

* * *

Questions for Reflection and Discussion

1. Explain the difference between *efficient* and *effective*. Give an example.

2. Think of an area of your life where more efficient working didn't produce the expected results.

3. Can you identify one or two important activities that are being squeezed out by some that are only urgent?

4. List several important goals you have set. How well are you progressing toward meeting them?

5. To what extent do you feel that your priorities need to be reordered at this point?

FIVE

How Is Your Time Being Used?

Though I am always in haste,
I am never in a hurry,
because I never undertake more work
than I can go through with calmness of spirit.
JOHN WESLEY

*O*nce we have our priorities clearly in view, we need to look at our present use of time (the actual use, not the ideal or intended one) to see how closely it matches our priorities. Only then can we schedule wisely so as to achieve our goals.

Step Two: Take Inventory
Some people feel that this step is unnecessary for them since they believe they already know how their time is being used. Paul, an engineering student who attended my seminar on this subject, was one of them. A month later he wrote me this letter:

> At the seminar I was sure I knew how my time was being used. But after a few days I decided to give the inventory a try. I was astonished by the result. I usually played a "few minutes" of pool after supper to relax before a long evening of study. I thought I was spending about half an hour a day. But the inventory showed

eight to ten hours a week! I could hardly believe it, but I couldn't evade the hard data. So I decided to keep closer control of a recreation that is needed but has been taking far more time than necessary. In doing so I freed about six hours a week in my busy schedule to be used for more important activities.

Paul's experience illustrates two kinds of time: outer and inner. External time measured by the clock is the same for all. Internal time experienced by the individual is often quite different. When we are doing something we enjoy, the time is all too short; we say that it flies. On the other hand, when have to do something we dislike, it seems endless; we say that the time drags.

For that reason, the way we feel about our activities is not an accurate gauge of how long they take. We need to know how our time is actually being spent now, in order to make realistic changes for more effective living. A record of past time usage provides the basis for influencing the future.

On this point we can benefit from a parallel between hours and dollars—the expenditure of time and money. People in financial difficulty, often with too many charge cards, sometimes go to a financial counselor. They expect to be told right away how to balance their budget and stay out of debt. So they may be surprised when the first step is not to make an ideal budget of how they *should* spend their money. Rather they are asked to account for where their dollars *are* being spent at present.

So it is with the process of budgeting your time. First you need to discover how you are currently using your hours. This step is essential because your pattern of activity reflects your lifestyle— not only its goals and values but also personal desires and needs. Changes in your present schedule, some of which can be painful, must begin with current reality. We are not all mind and muscle; much of our activity is influenced by emotional factors. For example, "workaholism" is hardly overcome simply by striving to adopt more efficient work habits.

Even though, like Paul, you may think you don't need this step, why not try it for a period of time? You too may be in for some surprises.

Chart Your Week

At the outset we need to ask, "Where do we start, with what period of time?" Many time-management techniques—like Ivy Lee's—focus on daily planning. For this choice there is a rationale. The day is the shortest natural unit of time, determined by the sun's rising and setting. Divided into hours, the day can be planned for the required activities. Those left undone can usually be scheduled for the following day. Daily planning is useful, as we will see in the following chapter.

But making the day our basic period tends to keep us focused on the urgent tasks, often diverting our attention from those that are important. So our basic planning period will be the week. Our society recognizes this time unit as the basis for organizing our activities. Business, industry, government and education operate within the framework of the week for work and time off.

Our Judeo-Christian tradition on this score goes back to the Genesis 1 account of creation. There God's creative activity is described in terms of six days, followed by a day of rest. That pattern became the basis for the Jewish week prescribed in the fourth commandment: "Remember the Sabbath day by keeping it holy. . . . [The Lord] rested on the seventh day" (Ex 20:8, 11).

This pattern of work and rest was continued by the early church in the form of Sunday, which eventually pervaded the Western world. Today most people think in terms of the week for scheduling their lives to include leisure and renewal of various kinds. Within this framework the Ivy Lee method of prioritizing activities already on the daily schedule can be useful. Longer-range planning can take account of monthly and annual priorities. But here we focus on getting a record of activities for a week.

Write It Down!

It's important to keep a record of your activities during a fairly typical week. (See figure 3.) For each day there is a column of half-hour sections between the time you rise and the time you go to bed. Those segments are sufficient for our purposes. Shorter periods would complicate the task, while the longer period of an hour would not be precise enough.

For one week, keep track of everything you do. Fill in every section of every day! If you have a job with regular hours, block out those hours at the beginning of the week; they require a separate evaluation. Before you turn out the light at night, be sure that each segment of the day is accounted for—meals, telephone, reading, church activity, shopping and so on. If an activity is interrupted, for example with a lengthy phone call, estimate the amount of time to the nearest half-hour and include it.

At the end of the week, count the hours spent in each activity and compare the totals with the list of priorities you made in step one. Brace yourself for a shock. Most of us, like Paul, will discover significant gaps between our high-priority activities and how much time we are actually spending on them.

> *Count the hours spent on each activity and brace yourself for a shock.*

You may wonder, *What can I do to rectify this situation? My schedule is already too full!* Before we answer that question in chapter six, we need to look at the chart from a different perspective. So far our inventory tells us only the *quantity* of time spent on each category. But what about the *quality* of the activity? That question leads us to look at two contrasting meanings of the word *time.*

Two Kinds of Time

In daily life we speak of time as a measurable quantity—a length of time such as a minute or hour, day or week, month or year. This meaning indicates the duration of activities that continue for a period. On other occasions, however, we focus on the quality—a special event or situation that we consider good or bad, right or wrong, favorable or unfavorable. We say, "Everyone had a really good time at the party." Here we are talking about not the chronology but the content.

For example, our senator in Washington is planning to run for reelection but has not yet made the decision public. In view of her interest in national educational policy, it appears that an invitation to lecture at our state university could be arranged. Two questions then arise: (1) How much time is available in her crowded schedule? (2) Is this a favorable time to launch her campaign?

This significant distinction is observed throughout the Bible, which has nearly a thousand references to time. Prominent are durations of days, weeks, months, seasons, years. Also important are special occasions of opportunity, crisis, celebration.

The Old Testament writers have a keen interest in chronology—in Israel's past, present and future. Their linear view of history—with a purpose, a beginning and an end—makes them more time-conscious than any other nation. They also appreciate a qualitative view that values events such as the major feasts of commemoration, rejoicing and worship.

In the New Testament two common Greek words for time are *chronos* (fifty-four occurrences) and *kairos* (eighty-five occurrences). By and large they distinguish between the two meanings we have noted. *Chronos* refers primarily to measurement and duration of time; *kairos,* on the other hand, indicates an opportune occasion or event.

For God's people the passage of time is not a threat; it contains an element of hope because God is active in history. Through the prophet Jeremiah the Lord assures Israel, "I know the plans I have for you . . . plans to give you a hope and a future" (Jer 29:11). *Both the chronology and content of that promise were fulfilled in the coming of the Messiah.*

This distinction is vitally important for understanding our present use of time and planning for the future. So far our use of the weekly chart has focused on *chronos*—linear, measured time. We

	Sun	Mon	Tue	Wed	Thu	Fri	Sat
6:00 a.m.							
6:30							
7:00							
7:30							
8:00							
8:30							
9:00							
9:30							
10:00							
10:30							
11:00							
11:30							
Noon							
12:30 p.m.							
1:00							
1:30							
2:00							
2:30							

Figure 3.   One-Week Time Log.

Photocopying privileges granted.

	Sun	Mon	Tue	Wed	Thu	Fri	Sat
3:00							
3:30							
4:00							
4:30							
5:00							
5:30							
6:00							
6:30							
7:00							
7:30							
8:00							
8:30							
9:00							
9:30							
10:00							
10:30							
11:00							
11:30							
Midnight							

have dealt with this quantitative aspect by simply counting the hours spent on each major activity. Now we need to recognize the importance of *kairos*—quality time.

Go through your chart again and mark the activities that center in personal relationships. Note the basic difference between things and people. While we can often schedule the completion of a task, that closure is not the same with people. *Chronos* needs to be made available for *kairos* experience in building personal relationships— a never-ending process.

In the next chapter we will consider the role of clock and calendar in helping us schedule these two types of activities.

* * *

Questions for Reflection and Discussion

1. Can you think of an activity that you enjoy but that seems to be taking more time than it should?

2. What parallels do you see between the use of time and the use of money—between spending hours and spending dollars?

3. What is the main thing you notice as you look over the chart of your typical week?

4. To what extent are you taking into account the difference between quantity and quality time in relationships?

SIX

Clock & Calendar: Friends or Enemies?

The clock, not the steam engine,
is the key machine of the industrial age.
LEWIS MUMFORD

A few years ago I visited Mexico City for the first time. My main purpose was to meet with committed Christian professors who were concerned for an effective witness to Jesus Christ within the university. Several days after my arrival the director of El Compañerismo Estudiantil, the Mexican sister movement to Inter-Varsity Christian Fellowship, arranged a free day to drive me south of the city to see the ancient pyramids.

Around midafternoon we started our return home for a visit from a professor at the university. About halfway my host surprised me by stopping in a beautiful little town for something to eat. I was enjoying the leisurely break until I looked at my watch. A quick calculation showed that we were an hour late for our five o'clock appointment! Yet my host seemed unperturbed.

As we resumed our drive and neared the city, the notorious traffic engulfed us and gradually slowed to a crawl. We were now even farther behind schedule. I had a vision of the professor impatiently waiting for our arrival and wondering whether he should go on home. Eventually I decided this wasn't my problem; I should stop worrying about the time and enjoy the sights.

We finally reached home about seven o'clock—two hours late. To my surprise the professor was not yet there. He soon arrived and, without apology, explained that an important faculty meeting had become overheated and had run much longer than expected. Yet now there would be no need to hurry our conversation—for him, as well as for us, dinner would be at the customary time, about nine o'clock.

This experience raised important questions: How late is late? What determines whether a person can be expected to arrive on schedule? It was evident that Mexicans operated on a different basis from the one I was used to.

Along with many other cultures around the world, Mexicans have an "event-oriented" view. Social and business occasions are expected to begin with the arrival of the key person—whatever that time may be. For example, at a banquet in the Philippines the main course may be served "on time" by the clock. Yet it may remain untouched and grow cold pending the "timely" arrival of the guest of honor. "Early" and "late" are determined not by the clock *(chronos)* but by a special event *(kairos)*.

In our American culture, however, activities are scheduled and run by the clock. They are expected to begin and end as planned. A major commandment, if not one of the Ten, is "Thou shalt not be late." For business or pleasure a person is expected to be prompt—at least within a few minutes. Yet in our relativistic age even that absolute appears to be giving way; punctuality now seems to be defined as the art of guessing how late the other person is going to be.

People and Things

The Philippine banquet illustrates the difference between people and things. There the primary focus was on the *diners*. American guests would be more concerned about the *dinner*—getting cold and less tasty.

In evaluating our present use of time and planning future activities, we need to be aware of the significant difference between primarily *working with people* and *working on things*. Following are several contrasting characteristics.

People	Things
Personal relationship	Impersonal view
Principles	Techniques
Effectiveness	Efficiency
Empowerment	Production
Cooperation	Performance

In dealing with people and things we should observe an important principle: "The worker is more important than the work." Obviously the worker is expected to do the assigned work. At the same time we need to keep in mind the welfare of the person.

By the way, this is how God feels about us: *who we are is more important to God than what we do.* Our well-being is of value to him. For his people God planned the sabbath, a day of rest just as important as their six days of work. Later we will look at the place of leisure in the Christian life.

In the wide variety of our activities with people, we need to recognize that the bottom line is personal relationship. On one occasion a Pharisee lawyer tried to test Jesus. "Teacher, which is the greatest commandment in the Law?"

Jesus replied, "Love the Lord your God with all your heart and with all your soul and with all your mind. . . . Love your neighbor as yourself" (Mt 22:34, 37, 39).

On your weekly chart you have entered your activities that involve other people. For each one, note the relationship (family, friend, colleague), situation (home, neighborhood, church), kind of desired activity (recreation, hobby, service project) and frequency (daily, weekly, monthly). If the activity is monthly, it may not be scheduled for the particular week chosen for inventory. In that case it requires special consideration on a longer-range basis. Sooner or later, however, it will appear on a weekly schedule.

This area of relationships calls for effectiveness and not efficiency. Getting more done with less effort is not the point here; connecting meaningfully with another person is what counts. Such a connection may be inefficient in the amount of time and energy required, but it is important. Quality time, not simply quantity time, is the goal.

For example, even a twenty-minute visit to a friend in the hospital for emergency surgery—during lunch hour, squeezed out of a busy day at the office—can be adequate evidence of loving concern. On the other hand, twenty minutes would hardly be "quality time" for an overdue visit to a friend who is struggling with a marriage in distress and needs a caring listener.

Now look at the activities and tasks that have already secured slots on your schedule. Compare them with the important items you started with, your goals and objectives. Question any that don't help you meet a goal of some sort. Can the activity be curtailed, like Paul's pool game, or phased out if not immediately discontinued? In the next chapter we will look at the art of saying no.

Step Three: Budget the Hours

At the outset reaffirm a fundamental reality: You cannot reorganize your life from square one. On this point many "time management" programs make a major mistake. They assume that you can sit down with a blank page or form and work out a totally new schedule to achieve the goals you have defined. Behold, the New You!

But in reality it is not possible to live a new schedule immediately. Your current pattern of activities is complex. For better or worse, it reflects interrelated demands, habits and satisfactions developed over many years. Some of them will hang on tenaciously. Like politics, *self-improvement is an "art of the possible" step by step.*

Imagine that you are sitting on the beach at the ocean, watching the whitecaps. Along comes a thirty-foot speedboat with a 100 hp motor. Suddenly it turns ninety degrees—in a matter of seconds. The new course is immediate and obvious to its passengers, clutching the rail and catching their breath.

Then in the distance you spot an ocean liner. As your eyes follow it, this vessel also turns. However, it behaves much differently. In order to make that course change, the captain signals a rudder move of only a few degrees. The great ship now turns so gradually that the hundreds of passengers hardly notice. In fact, only after you have watched it for quite a time do you begin to see the new course evident from the long curve of the ship's wake. If the captain had ordered a "hard starboard" in order to turn like the speedboat, the ship would have torn itself apart at the seams. Its ninety-degree turn would have been downward, bow first, to the bottom!

Our lives are like the ocean liner. We need to make our course changes by degrees. So start with the way you are using your hours now, and *plan small changes* as they become possible for you. Our Lord is an understanding teacher who helps us learn one lesson at a time. He will help you stay afloat.

Select one high-priority activity for which more time needs to be budgeted. Then make the hard decision as to what activity must be cut back or eliminated to provide the required hours. If it is a project or program for which you are still needed, its curtailment may have to be phased out. The main point is the tradeoff. It isn't a matter of squeezing the new activity into the cracks and crevices of an already full schedule.

For example, if you do not now have a daily time of Bible reading and prayer, decide to set the alarm ahead fifteen to twenty minutes. If you have trouble waking up, plan an earlier time to retire. You may have too many evening activities; if that is the case select one or two for discontinuing as soon as you can make a graceful exit. The resulting available time will provide an opportunity for reflection on the day's activities.

A Short History of the Clock

The clock as we know it was probably invented in the thirteenth century and first placed in public buildings. Until then monastery bells announced times for waking and retiring, prayers, meals, work and worship. Those early clocks had only hour hands and were not very accurate.

During the Renaissance and Reformation the use of clocks spread in several directions. They were significant in the new emerging science. They also appeared in the homes of the affluent to be admired as ornaments. For their owners clocks were more artistic status symbols than reliable instruments.

In the eighteenth century, accurate clocks became essential in commerce, especially for ocean navigation in flourishing world trade. Growing numbers of business people purchased clocks. By 1800, pocket watches were common among people in professions and trades. The first wrist watch was made by the Swiss in 1865; within a decade American factories were turning them out by the thousands.

The nineteenth century witnessed a profound change in the role of clocks that revolutionized society. At first they had simply facilitated the natural rhythms of everyday life based on the rising and setting of the sun. Now, however, with the industrial revolution clocks regulated individual lives and coordinated the activities of large groups in society.

From the outset, improved time-keeping devices have been opposed as well as accepted. Critics

You may now want to follow the same procedure for another important task or responsibility that is not getting enough time. But hold off on additional items until you have put the first one or two through the entire process.

One by one, the encouragement of modest successes will motivate you to stick with the process. As you fill in your schedule, reserve some time free each week for an emergency. Hours, like dollars, need to be set aside for unexpected demands.

Living by the Clock

Before we go on to implementing our new plans, we need to clear away misconceptions about that much-maligned timekeeper, the clock. For example, some social scientists charge that the clock represents an element of tyranny in modern life more potent than any other machine.

This judgment seems to be true in daily life. Most mornings an alarm clock, with buzz or beep, rouses us from sleep. The clock, in some form, keeps an eye on us throughout the day from dressing and breakfast through travel, work and evening activities, until bedtime. The clock's most frequent message is that we are behind schedule.

    Much of the criticism is based on misunderstandings of the role of the clock and the meaning of time. We have seen that time is simply a measure of activity, of motion and bemoan their use to control life: precision for the machinery and punctuality for the people. This view of living by the clock is satirized in Lewis Carroll's *Alice in Wonderland*. There the White Rabbit forever consults his pocket watch in order to avoid being late.

change. The clock indicates the "passage" or "lapse" of time. Neither the clock nor time *do* anything, good or bad; they simply keep track of activities that we have chosen.

    In this respect there is a parallel to the thermometer. It simply measures temperature, which in itself is neither good nor bad. It all depends on what is being measured. For example, a temperature of 105 degrees can be bad news as a symptom of illness; on the other hand, it may be a good sign of a chemical reaction in the laboratory.

    In ancient Greece it was customary to kill the messenger who brought bad news. Equally misguided is condemnation of the clock because we do not like what it reports. (At least we do not yet see a book entitled *The Tyranny of the Thermometer.*)

    In fact, the calendar and the clock can be good partners in providing tools for a meaningful life. The calendar looks forward to the future with a schedule of activities based on estimated times for their completion. The clock records the time that is actually being spent and indicates adjustments to the schedule that may be necessary. Hand in hand the wise use of these tools protects the planned activities from being crowded out by urgent but less important demands.

    The calendar prescribes the boundaries of our playing field and calls the plays to move the ball toward the goal. The clock monitors the activity and warns when the time is "running out." Within the rules of the game, we are free to use our skills and achieve our goals.

    Like any tool or technology, the calendar and clock can be misused. They become tyrants when used by others to impose on us activities that steal our hours for their own benefit. On the other hand, living by the clock under the lordship of Jesus Christ offers freedom to do his will.

Yet an important question remains: How can we keep on schedule to fulfill our commitments, guarded from encroachments and diversions?

* * *

Questions for Reflection and Discussion

1. In your life, what activities count as "special event" time rather than ordinary "clock" time?

2. How does the contrast between people and things open a window into your activities?

3. For an important activity that needs more priority, where can you find the additional time?

4. Small changes are important. Note one or two small steps you can take now.

SEVEN

The Art
of Saying
No

Simplicity, simplicity, simplicity!
I say, let your affairs be as two or three,
and not a hundred or a thousand;
instead of a million count half a dozen,
and keep your accounts on your thumb nail.
HENRY DAVID THOREAU

*S*hortly after dinner on a Monday evening, Janet's telephone interrupts her viewing of the evening news. A familiar voice makes an urgent request: "Can you lead the youth group meeting Wednesday evening? I've suddenly been called out of town on business and need a substitute." The pleading voice stresses the importance of this meeting and how well qualified she is to lead it.

Janet wonders how to handle this request. She has already planned her evenings throughout the week. Each one is important, but especially Wednesday. After many postponements because the task isn't urgent, Janet has finally reserved this evening for study and evaluation of a new job possibility. Yet the youth assignment is also important. She wonders, *How do I arrive at the right decision?*

Step Four: Implement the Plan

Even the best-laid plans produce little without a firm resolve to implement them. At the outset of each day, recommit yourself to the Lord as you think of the hours ahead. Then proceed through your schedule step by step. Keep track of the time you actually spend on each task. If you discover a tendency to underestimate it, you can take that into account in future planning.

Pray for wisdom in coping with any sudden demand on your time. It may be important enough to warrant a change in your plans. Or it may be a request you need to decline. First, *evaluate the proposed task* in terms of its urgency (a matter of timing) and its importance (a matter of value).

Sometimes a call for immediate attention is not all that significant for the caller. It turns out to be a sheep in wolf's clothing! On the other hand, the assignment can be important, as in Janet's situation. In that case the decision is more difficult. To escape the tyranny of the telephone she should take the following steps.

1. Resist pressure for an immediate answer. Avoid the tyranny of the telephone by informing the caller that you need time to check your schedule and pray about the possibility. In this case, you might say you can call back in half an hour. If you withstand the urgency of the moment, you can weigh the cost and discern whether the task is God's will for you.

2. Check your calendar or appointment book. If you accept this unexpected assignment, what scheduled activity must be curtailed or eliminated to make room for it? God may want you to accept the invitation, but not without first counting the cost. In Janet's case, she needs to weigh the importance of this job evaluation which has been neglected. It will have implications for the future long after the youth meeting, which probably can be led by someone else.

3. Call back. If your decision is no, explain with empathy but without apology that a previous commitment keeps you from accepting. You don't have to explain or defend that activity to the caller to justify your decision. Although you regret not being able

to meet this important need, you should not feel guilty.

P.S. After the event you may ask the caller, "How did the meeting go?" Invariably you will hear, "Fine. We got someone else who did a great job!" What a humbling experience. Over many years I have never heard anyone say, "Too bad—because you couldn't come, we had to cancel the meeting."

"Just Say No" to Urgency

Turning down an urgent request like the one Janet received is rarely easy. But it can be done gracefully and confidently when you remember this important truth: *You are the indispensable person only until the moment you say no.*

In recent years the slogan "Just Say No!" has become a "politically correct" antidote to growing addictions that increasingly endanger our society. Do we have problems with substance abuse, teenage pregnancy, violence, gambling, overeating? Persuade the addicts to just say no. But while this slogan may salve society's conscience, it hardly saves sufferers from their addictions. First the nature of the malady must be understood.

One of the most insidious enemies of a balanced, effective life is the element of urgency. Like fire, it can be a good servant but makes a bad master. Urgency is often needed in crises of life and death: a telephone call to the police, an ambulance ride to the hospital, warning of a possible bomb threat.

> *I have never heard anyone say, "Because you couldn't come, we had to cancel the meeting."*

On the other hand, urgency can be a counterfeit of importance; as such, its compelling call for immediate action is deceiving. The urgent task is rarely worthless; in its place it may be of some value. But when continuing to replace more important activities, it becomes a tyranny from which we need to be liberated.

It is sometimes suggested that urgency—"acting habitually or compulsively"—can be an addiction. As a practice, urgency has addictive features such as temporarily meeting a need, giving a sense of accomplishment, enhancing sense of self-worth, yet also increasing the problem it seeks to solve.

In this situation a person consistently sets aside the day's schedule to attend to urgent matters that are not important. Several factors—in society at large and in the individual—contribute to this habit.

The resulting busyness provides status in our society. People expect us to be busy, even overworked. Setting aside our own tasks to help others meet a deadline or crisis makes us appreciated, popular. In that activity we gain a sense of security.

Another factor also works against our saying no to an urgent request for help. As Christians, we feel an obligation to be a good Samaritan. Yet we must realize that *the need itself, however urgent, is not necessarily a call for us to meet it.* The need may be an occasion to do what the railroad signs command: "stop, look and listen"—and to be open to changing our plans if necessary. But the call for us to act must come from the Lord, who knows our limitations (Ps 103:13-14).

A fundamental factor in an individual's "productivity pattern" is the basic satisfaction gained through certain kinds of tasks. Among a wide variety of possible satisfactions are the following examples:

☐ Make Function or Effective: You like to fix something that is broken or needs to work better.

☐ Meet a Challenge or Test: You like to perform a difficult task, solve a problem, meet a deadline.

☐ Satisfy Expectations, Meet Human Needs: You like to follow instructions, help people in need.

☐ Influence Behavior, Gain Response: You like to affect activities, secure reaction, cooperation.

A person's basic satisfaction, in itself, is neither good nor bad; it is a gracious gift from God to be used for his glory. Yet satisfaction needs to be gained under the lordship of Christ. If, for example, your characteristic is one of the above, be alert. Know in advance that you will be more attracted to urgent pleas (and will have a more difficult time saying no) in this category. Understanding the dynamics of your specific pattern can help you guard against attractive diversions from your present responsibilities. (In the coming days, keep track of which urgent demands fall in this category to see if there is a correlation.)

Urgency itself is not the problem; on occasion urgency can be a prod to help you accomplish more quickly a task that is important to you. The danger light flashes when urgency becomes a dominant factor in your responses to requests for your time.

Impulse Spending

So far we have dealt with the problem of urgent requests coming to us from others. Another kind of pressure on the schedule is internal—desires of our own. What happens when the impulse to set aside the schedule is generated by ourselves? The issue may be clearer if we draw a parallel with our finances.

Ways to Say No

1. AVOID DESPERATE REQUESTS for your time by making a policy never to say yes to anything right away, before praying and consulting your calendar.

2. SCREEN PHONE CALLS when necessary, to give yourself time to revisit your priorities.

3. SUGGEST SOMEONE ELSE who could do the job and would enjoy the opportunity.

4. PUT A LIMIT on what you say yes to, and then stick to it when pressured to do more ("We thought as long as you were driving kids to the retreat you wouldn't mind staying to cook dinner").

5. RATION YOUR TIME and energy. If you plan to lead a Bible study this fall that takes two hours a week in preparation and two hours for the discussion and chatting afterward, you may need to postpone signing up to assist at the homeless shelter. Pick up that opportunity after the Bible study ends.

6. GO WITH YOUR GIFTS. Perhaps you are being pressured to join the church's finance committee *and* to head up the welcome ministry. You don't have room in your schedule for both tasks. Choose the one where you can do the better job; decline the other.

7. REAFFIRM THAT YOU SHOULD NOT FEEL GUILTY about saying no when the task is not one the Father is giving you to do.

Today most stores honor at least one credit card. This availability makes shopping as easy as flashing a VISA. It makes no difference to the system whether a purchase is a necessity on your list or an impulse of the moment. Yet a day of reckoning comes at the end of the month. Your bills may show a record of expenditures that far exceeds what you had planned. Unless paid in full, the debt begins to incur a high interest rate. There is no free lunch. The only way to escape the spiraling cost is to tighten your belt and begin to schedule repayment of the debt—without incurring more. That process often postpones or even eliminates items of actual need.

Both money and time are subject to "impulse spending." Some of us can resist spur-of-the-moment expenditures of our money but are not equally careful with our time. We can spend hours yielding to the impulse of a personal desire disguised as a need. Then, as some important task remains unfinished, we complain that our time has flown away.

It may be an interesting TV program not on your schedule, a long telephone conversation with a friend or extra time reading a magazine. Whatever the activity, it can be an impulse diverting energy from an important task that must find its place on a future schedule or go undone.

Occasional diversions are hardly fatal. In fact, they may be useful from time to time as evidence that delivery from a tyranny of the urgent isn't becoming *tyranny of the schedule*. Nevertheless, it is important to recognize our decisions and activities for what they are so that we can make midcourse corrections when necessary.

For better or worse, we're in a society that lives and dies by the clock. The clock can hardly be turned back, much less discarded. And the calendar is essential for relationships as well as tasks in a complex culture. So let's make the most of them to maximize our potential.

Evaluating & Revising the Plan

DuPont's former President Greenwald observed the principle "One minute spent in planning can save several in execution." It's not decision-making itself that causes tension so much as trying to decide under the pressure of circumstances calling for immediate action. Those situations are fewer and less stressful when we have done our homework.

Our cycle of priorities, time inventory, schedules and follow-up goes on as feedback from the last step enables us to revisit the first one. Changing circumstances call for periodic revision of our priorities and the steps to implement them.

You will be greatly helped if you set aside one hour a week for evaluation. Jot down comments on the past, record any lessons God may be

> *One minute spent in planning can save several in execution.*

teaching you and review your plans for the coming week. How are you doing with keeping the use of your hours in line with what you have planned to do? Repeat the exercise of writing down a week's time usage. How does your latest inventory match up with who God wants you to be?

Also try to reserve a few hours each month for longer-range evaluation and planning that includes time in prayer. Ironically, the busier we get, the more we need these periods—and the less we seem able to schedule them.

Prayerful waiting on God is indispensable to effective service. Here we learn the truth about God, ourselves and the tasks he wants us to undertake. Christians who are too busy to stop, take spiritual inventory and receive their assignments from God may be productive. We may work day and night to achieve much that seems significant to ourselves and to others. But we don't complete the work God has for us to do.

When your budgeting resolve breaks down, take courage, regroup and press forward with your overall strategy. The apostle James assures us: "If any of you lacks wisdom, ask God, who gives generously to all" (Jas 1:5). God has given each of us a unique combination of ability, strength and opportunity. Will he not also give us the insight and power to use our time effectively for his glory?

Nothing substitutes for knowing that on this day, at this hour, in this place, we are doing the will of our Father in heaven. Only then, like our Lord on the night before his death, will we be able to say amid many unfinished tasks, "I have completed the work you gave me to do" (Jn 17:4). Then we can look forward to seeing our Lord and hearing him say, "Well done, good and faithful servant" (Mt 25:21).

* * *

Questions for Reflection and Discussion

1. Have you had a telephone call that put you in a situation like Janet's? If so, how did you handle the problem of two competing important tasks?

2. In what sense has urgency in some areas of your life become addictive?

3. Do you recognize a "basic satisfaction" (sense of achievement) that you gain in certain tasks you really enjoy? If so, list some of those tasks.

4. To what extent are you likely to do "impulse spending" of energy on unscheduled activities?

5. Can you set a time this week for evaluation of your present schedule and planning for the future?

EIGHT

Time Out!

*I do not treasure God's promise
in my understanding but in my heart.
God's Word must penetrate deep within us.*
DIETRICH BONHOEFFER

*T*he long basketball season was finally ending in the league championship game. The two teams were well matched with about the same number of wins and losses. Back and forth they exchanged a lead that was never more than a few points. But with five minutes to go the home team began to falter, giving up three unanswered baskets.

Suddenly the coach signaled for a time out. The whistle blew, the game clock stopped and the players came over to the bench. There the coach sketched a new strategy to capitalize on his team's strengths. When play resumed, the new formation took their opponents by surprise and soon closed the gap to a tie. In the final seconds a jump shot by the home team won the game and the championship.

The rules for some team sports provide a time out for the players to catch their breath, assess their strategy and make whatever changes are called for. Since the game clock stops during this period, there is no actual loss of playing time. A time out doesn't change the score, but it does provide respite from the pressure long enough for the team to decide how best to use its ability and strength during the remainder of the game.

This principle of taking time out to evaluate our progress and revise our goals and strategies accordingly also applies to our own lives. Our situation is much the same as in sports, with one major exception. In the game of life we cannot "stop the clock," whose hands keep on moving. As St. Augustine put it, "Time never takes time off." Yet the value of a personal time out is well worth the cost.

What is a personal time out? It's a period of time set aside, free from other activities, to review our priorities, assess our performance and make necessary changes in present tasks and future plans.

That last word is especially important for Christians, who confess Jesus Christ as their Lord. The kingdom of God is not a realm but a relationship; it is primarily the gracious rule of God in our lives. For that reason, the primary purpose of our time out (or "quiet time" as many call it) is to nurture our relationship with him.

In chapter two we saw how Jesus fulfilled his mission through listening to the Father, discerning the words to proclaim and the healings to perform. To do this our Lord reserved time alone with the Father. It was often inconvenient; sometimes he lost sleep; often others misunderstood. But he gave it top priority.

> *Just when you think you can't afford to take time out . . . that's when you need it most.*

Today we are increasing our speed in most dimensions of life—yet we have a decreasing sense of direction and goals. Movement seems to be an end in itself, stifling questions of who we are and where we are going. Prolific French writer Jacques Ellul expresses concern over the rise of viewing people as machines. He points out, "No one knows where we are going, the aim of life has been forgotten, the end has been left behind. Man has set out at tremendous speed to go nowhere." Yet most people have a fear of being quiet and having to face the future. They prefer activity.

Many Christians, busy serving God, are in this situation. Their relationship with him is more acquaintance than friendship. Friendship takes time to nurture. They have not heard directly from God, or even from themselves, for a long time. The pace of modern life and the pressures at home and work stifle relationships and spiritual life. We realize that we need adequate time with God, with others and with ourselves. Yet we wonder how we can arrange for it.

Basic to all our activities must be an overriding sense of purpose. We need to hear again the words of our Lord in the Sermon on the Mount: "But seek first his kingdom and his righteousness, and all these things will be given to you as well" (Mt 6:33). Our basic commitment is to discover and do the will of God. In this we find meaning for all our activities.

Make It Your Policy

The best way to make time with God a regular part of your life is simply to set a policy and then stick to it. Decide in advance when and where it will be: before breakfast in the living room? at night before turning the light out? It's so easy to find excuses:

☐ "I've had a cold—I'd better sleep in this morning."

☐ "The weather is so bad today, I'd better skip my quiet time and get an early start."

☐ "There's a special on *Nightline* . . ."

☐ "This *Time* cover story looks interesting—my prayers haven't been very effective lately anyway."

If you set a policy, you don't have to make the decision each day; just do it!

And reserving a specific time day by day for renewing your relationship with God deserves high priority. This is a lifelong process in which you "grow in the grace and knowledge of our Lord and Savior Jesus Christ" (2 Pet 3:18). It will also be a means of

guidance, as you try to find the will of God for decisions you have
to make and tasks that call for your help. As you progress along this
path, the tension between your inner-time and outward activity will
diminish.

Yet at this point many encounter a roadblock: at present they do
not have a quiet place and time available for regular morning
devotions. In that case, improvise. Do you drive to work in a car
equipped with a cassette or CD player? If so, start your commute
with a hymn or two, which become the basis for meditation and
prayer. Write a verse of Scripture on a 3" × 5" card and carry it with
you to meditate on and memorize while stuck in traffic or waiting
in line. Once or twice a week skip your usual lunch in order to fast
and pray.

In the following pages, focusing primarily on our private devotions, our "inner-time" relationship with God, we look at several
patterns of using Scripture and prayer in the practical circumstances
of life.

Five Questions

Many shy away from devotional reading of the Bible because they
are not sure where to start or what to expect. Most guides have a
few verses for the day, but some use the text mainly as a springboard
for the writer's comments. Although they can be helpful, there is
no substitute for going directly to the Scripture to hear God's timely
message for your individual situation.

If you do not have such a daily quiet time at present, one of the
New Testament Gospels or Epistles is a good place to begin. In ten
to fifteen minutes you can read slowly through a chapter, think
about its relevance to your life, and pray for yourself and others in
the day ahead.

Suppose one day you received an invitation from the president
for a personal conversation. Would you consider this primarily an
opportunity to tell him what you thought of his policies or to request
some action to meet an urgent need? Possibly. But you would hardly

enter the oval office talking about your own concerns. You would first listen to what he had to say about the purpose of the interview and the ground he expected to cover. In due course you would have an opportunity to respond and express some of your own interests.

Likewise, we need to start our time out by listening. We want first to hear what God has to say. In the words of the psalmist, "I will listen to what God the LORD will say; he promises peace to his people" (Ps 85:8). Here are five questions to keep in mind as you read.

1. Is there a command to obey? Throughout its sixty-six books, the Bible has many commands for a variety of situations. Most of them are words spoken by God specifically to his people. The Ten Commandments were given through Moses at Mount Sinai. The Gospels record many instructions that Jesus gave to his disciples. The last parts of Paul's letters apply the apostle's teachings in the form of commands for living.

In your reading for the day, you may run across a command that is particularly relevant to your life at this time and calls for action.

Since Jesus didn't have formal theological education, the Jewish leaders challenged his authority. Jesus replied, "If anyone chooses to do God's will, he will find out whether my teaching comes from God or whether I am speaking on my own" (Jn 7:17). This condition lies at the heart of Christianity: a decision to do the will of God. A resolve to obey Christ's teaching opens the door to knowing its truth and putting it into practice.

2. Is there a sin to confess and forsake? This is the other side of the coin: a call to *stop* doing something. The day's Scripture passage may illuminate a wrong attitude or action in your life. It may be a sin of which you have not been aware, or one with which you are now struggling. Either way, according to the apostle John, "If we confess our sins, he is faithful and just and will forgive us our sins and purify us from all unrighteousness" (1 Jn 1:9).

Confession is more than saying "I'm sorry." It involves a willingness to stop doing what is sinful. Another biblical word for this action is *repentance,* a turning around to go in the opposite direction. It is a resolve by God's grace and power to resist temptation when it appears. The psalmist expresses this essential: "If I had cherished sin in my heart, the Lord would not have listened" (Ps 66:18).

3. Is there an example to follow—or avoid? Although the Bible has many teachings about God and humanity, it is mainly history, a record of events. It is the story of individuals, families, tribes and nations. God the Creator and Sustainer of the universe is also the Lord and Judge of history. His revelation comes in mighty acts of mercy and judgment whose meaning is proclaimed by the prophets.

Rich in biographical information, the Bible offers many good examples to follow and bad examples to avoid. Sometimes both are prominent in the same person. David resisted an opportunity to take the life of his enemy King Saul. Later, when he was king, David took the wife of his faithful soldier Uriah,

> *The link between* hearing *and* doing *the will of God is* deciding *at the moment it is spoken.*

then had Uriah killed in battle. Today as you read you may sense that one example in particular is relevant to your life and calls for action.

4. Is there a promise to claim? If so, are there any conditions? The promises of God permeate both the Old and New Testaments. An example of the former appears in the Ten Commandments given to Moses: "Honor your father and your mother, so that you may live long in the land the LORD your God is giving you" (Ex 20:12). Continued enjoyment of their new country is contingent upon the people's obedience to God's laws.

A New Testament instance is found in the apostle Paul's letter to the Philippians. The promise of peace depends on their obedience. "Whatever you have learned or received or heard from me, or seen in me—put it into practice. And the peace of God will be with you" (Phil 4:9).

5. Is there a new thought about God—Father, Son or Holy Spirit? Even the most familiar Scripture passages have the potential for new insight. As well as you know Psalm 23, for example, today it can reveal an aspect of your Shepherd's care that you haven't experienced before. Has the psalm changed? No; it is your changing situation that opens you to this understanding, which inspires thanksgiving and praise.

It is unlikely that you will read very far in most parts of the Bible before at least one of these questions is relevant—except, of course, the long Old Testament genealogies and tabernacle details which are hardly recommended for daily devotions!

If the message calls for action in the coming days, how will you respond? Are you likely to say, "I'll have to think this over and see what happens"? But when the time for action arrives, your memory or resolve may have weakened. The delay may have lost the value of the time out for making decisions.

What would you think of the basketball team if the players simply talked about the situation during the time out?—then at the whistle went out on the court, under game pressure, to work out a new strategy?

The (often missing) link between *hearing* and *doing* the will of God is *deciding* at the moment it is spoken. When the decision has been made in advance, all that remains is to *do it* when the time comes.

Meditating on the Word

Relatively few Christians have learned to meditate on a passage of Scripture. One reason is cultural: Americans as a nation are hardly known for their meditation on anything. Another reason lies in the frequent linking of the practice to New Age, yoga, Zen and TM, often with a mantra to recite. But that connection should not rob us of the value of genuine scriptural meditation.

In everyday use the word *meditate* simply means "contemplate, reflect on, consider at length." Meditation is practiced and taught by the biblical writers. The book of Psalms begins by blessing those whose "delight is in the law of the LORD, and on his law [they] meditate day and night" (Ps 1:2). Psalm 119 uses the word *meditate* eight times. Each time the meditation focuses on the word of God: his precepts, decrees, laws, statutes. Its purpose is communion with the living God in covenant relationship.

Eastern mysticism, however, emphasizes detachment from the world, the loss of personhood in a merging with the Cosmic Mind. There is a longing to be released from the struggles and pains of this life. In its popular form, TM is more optimistic, a "meditation for the materialist." It is a method to improve your physical and emotional well-being without a required belief in the spiritual world. It is clear that these two different meanings of meditation are polar opposites.

In recent decades Christian meditation has become more widely appreciated. Especially influential has been the life and teaching of Dietrich Bonhoeffer, a brilliant German theologian and church leader who stood firm against Hitler's persecution of the Jews. In April 1943, Bonhoeffer was arrested, never again to be a free man. During the following two years he wrote *Letters and Papers from Prison.* Though never intended for publication, they have continued to exert a profound influence.

Bonhoeffer practiced a meditative reading of the Bible that shaped his Christian life, giving it direction and guidance. He urged a meditation "bound to Scripture" to guide our prayers and discipline our thoughts. He urged, "Accept the Word of Scripture and ponder it in your heart as Mary did. That is all. That is meditation" (*Meditating on the Word* [Boston, Mass.: Cowley Publications, 1986], p. 33).

Begin your meditation by praying to the Holy Spirit for concentration. Then turn to the biblical text. Ask of each passage, *What is God saying here?* Pray that he will help you hear what he wants to say—not just general truths but the will of God for you today. At the close of meditation, offer thanksgiving for whatever blessings you are aware of. Then, just as the words of a person dear to us follow us throughout the day, so the Word of Scripture will continue to work in you ceaselessly.

Dietrich Bonhoeffer describes this interaction between God's Word and our prayer.

The words that come from God will be the steps upon which we find our way to God. Grounded in the Scripture, we learn to speak to God in the language which God has spoken to us. We learn to speak to God as a child speaks to its mother. The entire Bible, then, is the Word in which God allows himself to be found by us. (p. 40)

Bonhoeffer felt a need of firm discipline for prayer. He recognized that we often pray according to our moods. So it is good to have a regular time and place early in the day.

We want to meet Christ in his Word. Meet him first in the day before you meet other people. . . . Before our daily bread should be the daily Word. Only thus will the bread be received with thanksgiving. Only thus will the work be done as the fulfillment of God's command. (p. 45)

> *"The words that come from God will be the steps upon which we find our way to God."*
> —*Bonhoeffer*

In the early morning on April 9, 1945, as World War II in Europe was ending, Dietrich Bonhoeffer was executed in Flossenburg concentration camp. The camp doctor reported his last hours (*Christianity Today,* April 3, 1995, p. 27):

Pastor Bonhoeffer, before taking off his prison garb, knelt on the floor praying fervently to his God. I was deeply moved by the way this lovable man prayed, so devout and so certain that God heard his prayer. . . . At the place of execution he again said a short prayer and then climbed the steps of the gallows, brave and composed. . . . I have hardly ever seen a man die so entirely submissive to the will of God.

That submission had begun many years earlier. Through meditation on the Word, step by step, Bonhoeffer found God's path for him and walked it in a life of faith, obedience and courage.

Put meditation into your schedule on a regular basis. You'll find that the perspective you gain will enable you to handle that schedule—and to handle all of life—better.

* * *

Questions for Reflection and Discussion

1. What place does a "time out" have in your schedule? If it has not been your habit, do you feel ready to try it during the next couple of weeks? If so, write down the time you will set aside.

2. Which of the five questions seem most relevant to your Bible reading? Look for answers to all five as you read in these next days.

3. What impresses you most about Bonhoeffer's comments on meditation and Scripture?

NINE

Following
the Lord

O Lord Jesus Christ, we pray you not to let us stray
from you, who are the Way, nor to distrust you,
who are the Truth, nor to rest in any other thing than you,
who are the Life. Teach us by your Holy Spirit what
to believe, what to do, and wherein to take our rest.
DESIDERIUS ERASMUS

When we have too many things to do and not enough time
to do them, or when we need to make an important decision about
our lives, we want God to show us the way. We ask ourselves, *How
can I receive God's guidance?*

"The answer is simple," one preacher explained. "Think about
how a captain is guided at night to steer his ship safely between
shoals into a harbor. He simply lines up the ship's bow with the
lights on three buoys leading to the dock. Similarly, God guides us
though the Scripture, our circumstances and the counsel of Christian friends. When those three line up the course of action is clear."

It all seems so simple, until a question clouds the formula.
Suppose dense fog rolls in to enshroud those buoys? What if the
three sources of guidance aren't visible?

I remember the time my two older sons and I sailed off the
southern Massachusetts coast and encountered such a fog. For years

we had sailed Narragansett Bay, Rhode Island, in various kinds of weather in our twenty-four-foot sloop with its small cabin. Now we were ready for a longer cruise—to Martha's Vineyard.

For the first few days the weather was good with a steady wind out of the southwest. Then small craft warnings told us to return to Rhode Island. By early afternoon the wind began to die. Was this a calm before a storm? We lowered useless sails and started our outboard motor. We had to reach the shelter of Cuttyhunk Harbor by nightfall.

Moving along the south coast of the Elizabeth Islands, we were able to cruise a few hundred feet from shore. By late afternoon the sun shone orange as it sank toward the horizon in a thickening haze. Then, without warning, the sun disappeared entirely. Off to starboard we could barely see the high cliffs. As the haze became fog my uneasiness turned into fear. I remembered stories of these islands enshrouded and ships wrecked.

As the fog thickened we steered closer and closer to the island. Fortunately the water was deep right up to shore. But at the western end of the island a small reef jutted out on one side of the narrow channel. At that point we would have to steer away from land and lose our sighting. With visibility down to a few feet, there was little chance of our seeing even the first buoy marking the sharp turn into the channel.

Soon we saw the white water and veered out into the dense fog where we were unable to take our bearing. As we prayed for guidance to safety, we suddenly saw something black across our bow. It proved to be the silhouette of a lobster boat that was apparently headed for the channel we could not see. The man at the helm made his living in these waters with all kinds of weather. He knew exactly where he was going.

I pointed our sloop in that direction and followed him. Never had a lowly lobster boat looked so good. In the gathering darkness we were just able to keep him in sight as he passed the first buoy near the mouth of the narrow channel. We barely glimpsed the other two as we slipped between the rocks into the safety of the harbor, now pitch black. Around midnight a forty-knot wind whistled in the rigging. We thanked God for the guidance of the lobster boat in our crisis of direction.

The following day dawned sunny with a brisk, steady wind. We anticipated a great sail back to Rhode Island. As our sloop left the harbor, I glanced astern toward the narrow channel. Silhouetted in the sunlight were the three buoys, useful guides—when they can be seen!

In retrospect, I realized that our experience with the fog at sea was an enacted parable about God's guidance. When our usual means of navigating had failed us, God provided direction. It came not in a formula or plan but through someone who knew the way and could be followed.

Yet we ask, *How can I know God's will for my life? What about important questions like career, job, marriage, in which I need to make a decision?*

To clear up confusion about this dimension of the Christian life, let's first look at Scriptures explaining the will of God for all Christians. We can then consider a variety of means by which we can be guided.

The Will of God

The Bible reveals God not only as Creator and Sustainer of the universe but also as Lord and Judge of history. He is actively involved in human affairs to fulfill the purposes for which he has created us.

The phrase "will of God" in various forms appears about sixty times in the Old and New Testaments. It connotes his desire for something to happen, his plans for individuals, families, nations. For example, in the Lord's Prayer we say, "Your kingdom come, your will be done on earth as it is in heaven" (Mt 6:10).

So what do we mean by asking *What is God's will for my life?* Often it expresses our concern mainly about an action of some kind—career, friendship, church or community service. But the answer lies in a broader context. It is not basically a question of what we are going to do, but who we are going to be.

First, God has revealed that he "desires everyone to be saved and to come to the knowledge of the truth" (1 Tim 2:4 NRSV). Repentance and faith lead to confession of Jesus Christ as Lord and Savior, to life under new management.

> *The Holy Spirit enables us to discern and live out the will of God.*

Second, the apostle Paul writes, "We instructed you how to live in order to please God. . . . It is God's will that you should be sanctified" (1 Thess 4:1, 3). In the Christian life character is primary. The essential is moral and ethical living with evidence of the fruit of the Holy Spirit. In this respect the will of God is the same for all believers.

The key to this kind of life appears in Romans 12:2: "Don't let the world around you squeeze you into its own mould, but let God remould your minds from within, so that you may prove in practice that the Plan of God for you is good" (JBP).

We need to resist the pressure to be shaped by our society's values and goals. Discovering the will of God is not limited to major life-changing decisions; it is something we do each day. Reading Scripture keeps fresh in our minds the commands to obey, promises to claim, sins to forsake. We are open to God's guidance even in the small choices. Day by day, through the power of the Holy Spirit, we discern and live out the will of God.

"Follow Me"

Questions about the will of God for our lives often bring to mind the concept of a plan or blueprint—something we either have or don't have but want. It may be a road map that shows how to get where we want to go. If the drive is long enough, our trusty AAA trip-tik will lay out the most desirable route. Between major cities it lists not only distances but travel hours required. So barring a flat tire or engine trouble, we can calculate to within a few minutes our estimated time of arrival. Once we have the map, we no longer need the person who provided it.

The biblical model of discipleship, however, is more like a day of fishing in an area of lakes and forests. From the outset an experienced guide leads us along barely visible trails through woods with no water in sight. Eventually we arrive at the shore of a lake, where the guide lays out the appropriate tackle and shows us where to use it. Finally we catch some fish! As the afternoon wanes, the guide leads us back. From start to finish he has been with us in this adventure.

Jesus used the fishing model in calling his first four disciples. As he walked beside the Sea of Galilee he saw Simon and his brother Andrew fishing. Jesus said, "Follow me and I will make you fish for people" (Mk 1:17 NRSV). Immediately they left their nets and followed him. A little later Jesus saw James and his brother John mending their nets; he gave the same invitation, to which they also responded.

Soon Jesus called eight additional disciples, listed in Matthew 10:2-4. After they had spent time with the Master, he sent the Twelve out to preach the kingdom of God and heal every kind of disease.

The command "Follow me" is central in Jesus' teaching. He declared, "If any want to become my followers, let them deny themselves and take up their cross and follow me" (Mt 16:24 NRSV). That invitation is often misunderstood in two ways. First, the denial is mistakenly thought to focus on certain practices or places that the Christian is expected to forego. It conveys a negative lifestyle of abstinence that can become a legalism. Second, the phrase "bearing my cross" is applied to a specific illness or other trial to be endured. Yet these difficulties are not voluntary; they afflict everyone in a fallen world.

Actually, Jesus' requirement for discipleship is more basic. *Bearing my cross* is essentially *denying my right to my own life.*

Those phrases are two ways of expressing the same principle. It is voluntary, a way of living that I choose. It is crossing out the vertical "I" of my own will with Jesus' prayer in Gethsemane: "Not my will, but yours be done" (Lk 22:42). That principle doesn't require perfection. Following Jesus, at any given time, means committing all I know of *myself* to all I know of *him*. That understanding allows for growth in both dimensions of the relationship.

Making Decisions

As we follow the Lord he is constantly working *in* and *around* us as well as *through* us. By the power of the Holy Spirit we are growing in grace, in the fruit of the Spirit. God is shaping our circumstances, sometimes in unusual ways. In our various activities, we seek wisdom for the daily decisions we face. Yet as we pray for guidance on a specific occasion we wonder how, very practically, it may be given. If not with a map or formula or procedure, how *do* we make our decision? It may be influenced by requirements, opportunities or difficulties involved in the situation. But ultimately the means of guidance—expected or not—comes from the Lord.

Over the years we realize that all decisions regarding our stewardship of time, possessions, money, relationships and activities call for willingness to practice the lordship of Christ in every area of life.

We can be grateful that God does guide our decisions and actions as we seek first his kingdom and path of service. God declares to his people, "I will instruct you and teach you in the way you should go; I will counsel you and watch over you" (Ps 32:8). The promise also comes through Isaiah: "I am the LORD your God, who teaches you for your own good, who leads you in the way you should go" (Is 48:17 NRSV).

But it is not by means of a standard procedure—not through formula but through friendship. Jesus said to his disciples, "I have called you friends" (Jn 15:15). God guides us in different and sometimes unexpected ways. If he did not, we would tend to reduce guidance to an impersonal system.

Sometimes family or job responsibilities call for a possible move to another part of the country. The counsel of a trusted friend who knows us well can open a window to a new perspective on a puzzling set of circumstances. Prayer and conversation help us sort out the pros and cons of the action we are considering.

At times a specific Scripture speaks clearly to an urgent and important decision we are facing. For example, look at the account of a rich young ruler who came to Jesus seeking eternal life. After a brief conversation the Lord said, " 'Go, sell what you own, and give the money to the poor, and you will have treasure in heaven; then come, follow me.' When he heard this, he was shocked and went away grieving, for he had many possessions" (Mk 10:21-22 NRSV).

Over the years many Christians, including myself, have heard this command as a specific word from the Lord. We have left behind, if not wealth, something of real value such as career or proximity to family. Every Christian on occasion is called to reevaluate something that can prove a roadblock to a new path of discipleship. How will you respond when you hear the Lord say, "Go . . . sell . . . give . . . come . . . follow me"?

As you face decisions you may not see three buoys neatly lined up. However, one of them can be enough to point you in the right direction, which may then be confirmed by others that appear as you move along. In that process the Holy Spirit works in and for you, to help you know the will of God and to guide you in the decision at hand.

A Risen Lord

As we experience different ways of being guided, we gradually get the picture. At first we viewed the process of Scripture reading, prayer and openness to the Spirit primarily as a *means* to an end: arriving at a decision. Our Lord, however, views the process itself as a *goal:* strengthening our relationship with him. The actual decision, in whatever way it may be reached, is mainly a byproduct.

If Jesus were not alive, we could not really "follow" him. Other religious leaders also teach a set of doctrines, a way to "salvation" of one kind or another. Disciples (learners) accept their leader's teaching and practice, but they cannot become his "followers" in a relational sense. We cannot follow someone who is dead—except into death.

In contrast, Jesus said to his disciples, "I am the way, and the truth and the life" (Jn 14:6). He died and rose again to be Lord of the living. In a real sense Christianity is Christ, whom we know and love and serve.

In the early years of InterVarsity Christian Fellowship in the United States, a small British IVF book by H. A. Evan Hopkins profoundly influenced many of us students. Its title, *Henceforth,* came from the apostle Paul's second letter to the church at Corinth:

> *Christianity is Christ, whom we know and love and serve.*

He died for all, that they which live should not henceforth live unto themselves, but unto him which died for them, and rose again. (2 Cor 5:15 KJV)

"No Reserve—No Retreat—No Regrets"

One particular chapter heading hit home: "No Reserve—No Retreat—No Regrets." The author described in practical ways what it means to confess, without reservation, "Jesus Christ is Lord." He commented on Jesus' warning "No one who puts a hand to the plow and looks back is fit for the kingdom of God" (Lk 9:62 NRSV). He also explained that "no regret" doesn't mean no sins and failures to confess. It does mean no disappointment or distress over the decision to follow this call of Christ.

"No Reserve—No Retreat—No Regrets." I could not imagine a better lifelong motto than this one, for my life and yours.

* * *

Questions for Reflection and Discussion

1. How has God guided your decisions at crucial points—opportunity, crisis, fork in the road?

2. Is there an area of your life in which you now feel "squeezed into this world's mold"?

3. In what area of your own life have you heard Jesus' call to "go . . . sell . . . give . . . come . . . follow"?

4. How would you explain to someone the importance of Christ's resurrection in your life?

TEN

No Time Like the Present

On my calendar there are but two days:
today and That Day.
MARTIN LUTHER

*A*round six a.m. the telephone jarred me into consciousness. Who could be calling so early in the morning? My mother's voice a thousand miles away reported, "Your father had another heart attack in the night and died a short while ago."

The news was a shock. When I visited my parents two months earlier, he had seemed healthy with no signs of recurrent illness.

On my flight east, I wondered how my mother was coping with this sudden loss. As the oldest son I would be expected to comfort her and other family members. I had no idea of what that would mean; the usual words seemed hollow.

But from the moment of my arrival I found that my mother was the source of strength. It was she who eased the pain of the others and made the necessary decisions. In her greatest loss an unwavering trust in the Lord was evident. And it persisted throughout the remaining fifteen years of her life as a widow.

I realized that my mother's faith and strength in this crisis were the fruit of a lifelong relationship with her Lord. As far back as I could remember she had daily read her Bible and lived its message. Her confidence in God had persevered through many trials, including economic depression, family deaths and the overseas wartime service of two sons. For her there was *no time like the present* to meet life's challenges and be ready for the future.

In this last chapter we will consider the importance of the present time and task in the example and teaching of two remarkable Christians whose influence has persisted through three centuries. We will finally focus on the future that awaits all who know and serve our God.

Past and Future

Although we concentrate on living in the present—the only life and time we have—memories of the past and hopes for the future influence our present activities.

We all know people who live in the past. Frequently they are elderly. Life with its major activities is drawing to a close. As strength is ebbing they look back, recalling both good and bad experiences.

For many, including the young and middle-aged, decisions of the past have led down some wrong path to disastrous consequences. Reliving that experience, years or even decades later, still stirs painful regret and self-condemnation. "If only I had not been so foolish . . . blind . . . stubborn." Yet, like the instant replay of a football game, no matter how many times memory reviews the event, the result is the same. That memory can continue to haunt and inhibit our present moments.

For painful, even crippling, memories there is inner healing through Jesus Christ, who preached and healed all kinds of sickness. He declared, "I have come that they may have life, and have it to the full" (Jn 10:10). Yet even though its memory is healed, the experience may still have present consequences.

A mistaken view of the future can also have harmful effects for the present. Most of us tend to expect that we will be better Christians in the future. For example, when we see a person ten or twenty years older than ourselves, whom we greatly admire, we think, *Of course, when I'm that old, I'll be like that: loving, kind, good, patient, faithful.* But our complacency crumples when we meet such a person our own age—or even younger! We realize that the passage of time itself has not changed us.

We are reminded by Thomas à Kempis (1388-1471):

Living a long time doesn't automatically make us better persons. Sometimes the years increase only our burden of guilt, not the quality of our behavior. It would be wonderful if we could live even one day well. Many can tell you the date of their conversion, but their lives have little to show for it.

Another form of false hope expects that some future opportunity or crisis will suddenly empower us. That it will put into us the courage and strength to "rise to the occasion." Yet when a crisis crashes into our life, perhaps a serious accident or death in the family, our faith can falter. Words fail us; we have no comfort or wisdom to give.

We realize too late that the crisis itself doesn't build into us what is needed; it only brings out what is (or is not) already there. The opportunity does not infuse us with new

> *We have only today, this hour, within our grasp.*

character; it simply provides the occasion to demonstrate what we have become day by day. In time of war, for example, the battlefield rarely *makes* heroes and cowards; it simply *reveals* them. Sometimes it is the least likely soldier who unexpectedly leads other members of his platoon into fierce enemy fire.

We need to live in the present, neither dragged down by the past nor distracted by the future's problems or promises. Fugitives into the past and the future have one thing in common: they have difficulty living effectively in the present. The past cannot be recovered, even though we can learn from it; the future is not yet ours, even though we prepare for it. The past lives only in our memories, the future in our imagination. So the present must become more than a bridge linking the past and the future. *We need to rediscover how to live in the present.* We have only today, this hour, within our grasp.

Two Remarkable Men

Two men who lived three centuries ago can teach us what this kind of living means. Although similar in some respects, they had radically different kinds of influence.

Both lived in France during the same general period. Their long lives overlapped about forty years: Jean-Pierre de Caussade (1675-1751) died at the age of 76, Brother Lawrence (1611-1691) at 80. The teaching of each was published after his death in a single brief volume consisting of a few letters coupled with notes taken by others of conversations and lectures. In both the central message is simple yet profound: *wholehearted commitment to God motivated by love—moment by moment, task by task.*

Yet the two men could hardly have been more different in education, social status and vocation. Jean-Pierre de Caussade was a university graduate with a doctorate in theology. During his long life he was a professor, administrator, pastor and mediator for the high and mighty in church and state. On the other hand, Brother Lawrence lacked formal education and served as a footsoldier in the devastating Thirty Years' War. During the latter part of his life he was a Carmelite lay brother who became the cook for his community.

The Sacrament of the Present Moment

For many years Jean-Pierre de Caussade served as director of the Visitation nuns in the splendid city of Nancy. Letters he sent to them combined with notes of talks he gave on retreats were carefully preserved. In 1861, about a century after his death, they were published in a book titled *Abandonment to Divine Providence.*

Since then the book has exerted an influence all out of proportion to its one hundred pages. A major reason is that Caussade expresses profound truth in practical, everyday language. He recognizes that most of us are very ordinary creatures with humdrum lives of trivial tasks and decisions: some pleasant, many boring, others tedious or tragic. Yet we need to recognize that God speaks through what happens to us. No matter how difficult they may be to understand, the events of each moment are stamped with the will of God.

The key to Caussade's message is this principle: "If we have abandoned ourselves to God, *there is only one rule for us: the duty of the present moment*" (*Abandonment to Divine Providence* [New York: Doubleday, 1975], p. 20). The past is past, the future is yet to be; we can do nothing about either. But we can deal with the present—what is happening moment by moment.

But, we may ask, what does that mean in practice day by day? Caussade spells out three kinds of duty: acceptance of present circumstances; performance of assigned tasks; response to prompting by the Holy Spirit.

1. Accept the will of God. He calls this the "sacrament of the present moment." A sacrament is defined as "a visible sign of an inward grace." We are to welcome all the present circumstances of our life as an expression of God's will. The apostle Paul affirms, "In all things God works for the good of those who love him" (Rom 8:28). This is not the passivity of fatalism but the activity of faith.

2. Perform assigned tasks. Basic is our obedience to the clearly expressed will of God for holy living: Christian character and moral action. Each day, then, we carry out the tasks assigned to us in whatever variety they may offer. "Leave everything to God except your love and obedience to the duties of the present moment" (p. 66).

3. Respond to the Holy Spirit. Caussade teaches a third kind of duty: "obeying those promptings with which God moves us who are submissive to him." It is not governed by rules but is under the control of the Holy Spirit. He may guide me to a person who needs advice from me, or he may guide me to ask some for myself. He gives us these words of life; all we say to others must come from him. For guidance in this way of living Caussade uses a nautical metaphor: "When the wind is shifting, one can be sure of its direction only from moment to moment" (p. 61).

Knowledge for Christian living comes through Scripture and experience. The latter is absolutely necessary if we are to touch the hearts of those to whom God sends us. Without the experience of being led by the Holy Spirit we are like dough without yeast or salt.

So we see that *acceptance* of God's will is not resignation but a positive embrace. Nor is *performance* of our assigned tasks a compulsive obedience but a labor of love. It is a *response* to the Holy Spirit, who empowers us in everything we do—planned or unplanned.

There is nothing more reasonable, more excellent, more holy than God's will. . . . If you are taught the secret of finding its presence in every moment of your lives, then you possess all that is most precious and supremely worthwhile. . . . The present moment is always overflowing with immeasurable riches. (p. 41)

The Presence of God

When he was converted to Christ at the age of eighteen, Nicholas Herman received a high view of God's providence and power that kindled in him a burning love. At the age of fifty-five he was admitted as a lay brother among the Carmelites Dechausses (bare-footed) at Paris, where he served in the community kitchen. He then became known as Brother Lawrence.

Soon his spiritual influence reached the ears of M. Beaufort, grand vicar to Cardinal de Noailles, who visited him on August 3, 1666. There must have been something unusual in a monastery cook to warrant that visit by a high official. In the first of four conversations over several months, Brother Lawrence reported how his spiritual life had been established on that high view of God. After that his only concern was to perform all his actions for the love of God.

At the close of this conversation the official must have been surprised when the cook, a model of humility, concluded his comments by saying, "If it is your purpose sincerely to serve God, you may come as often as you desire, without any fear of being troublesome. But if not, you should not come back" (*The Practice of the Presence of God* [Cincinnati, Ohio: Forward Movement Publications, 25th printing, p. 7).

The grand vicar went home and made notes of the conversation. And on September 28 he did come back for three more visits. The reports of Brother Lawrence's comments, comprising eighteen pages, and sixteen brief letters were published a year after his death in February 1691. The title is based on Brother Lawrence's key statement: "If I were a preacher, above all other things I should preach *the practice of the Presence of God*" (pp. 26-27). Since then the original French has been translated into many languages.

Yet we may ask, "What does this mean? How do we go about it?" Brother Lawrence would be the last to provide a procedure or promote a method. He tells us that he read many books offering a variety of practices, only to become puzzled and discouraged. So he resolved simply "to give myself up to God, as the best return I could make for his love" (p. 31). He then shares how this commitment works out in daily life.

1. Commitment to the will of God. The high view of God, motivated by love, calls for unreserved commitment to fulfilling his will, whether in suffering or consolation. Here is a reflection of the apostle Paul's urging us to "offer your bodies as living sacrifices, holy and pleasing to God" (Rom 12:1).

Brother Lawrence warns that "we ought to make a great difference between the acts of the *understanding* and those of the *will*" (p. 11). The crucial issue in Christian living is not mental assent but obedient action. In fact, according to our Lord a desire to do the will of God is the key to knowing the truth (Jn 7:17).

2. *Conversation with God.* Practicing the presence of God involves our growing awareness that God is intimately present with us. Brother Lawrence points out that we establish a sense of God's presence by continually conversing with him. "We ought to act with God in the greatest simplicity, speaking to him frankly and plainly, and imploring his assistance in our affairs, just as they happen." In

> *The value of an action lies not in its size but in its motive—love for God.*

this conversation we are also "praising, adoring and loving him continually for his infinite goodness and perfection" (p. 13).

For Brother Lawrence the set times of prayer are not different from other times since he continues with God in those activities. For him prayer is not an escape from the world, a "sacred" period removed from daily life. Those tasks, performed with a motive of love, are themselves a form of prayer.

3. *Activities of daily life.* How then does Brother Lawrence go about his "common business," such as his kitchen work to which he naturally has great aversion? At the outset he prays that God will give him the grace to continue in his presence and to succeed in his tasks. As he proceeds with his work he continues his conversation with his Maker, enjoying the presence of God.

His example of peace under pressure has been more influential than his words. He reports that "in the noise and clatter of my kitchen, while several persons are at the same time calling for different things, I possess God in as great tranquility as if I were upon my knees at the blessed sacrament" (p. 20).

4. *Sins and failures.* But what about shortcomings from which even the godly are not free? Lapses in devotion, a wandering mind, failure to ask for assistance? Brother Lawrence is clear: "We ought without anxiety to expect the pardon of our sins from the blood of Jesus Christ, only endeavoring to love him with our whole hearts. . . . We should pray for his grace with a perfect confidence" (p. 11).

We should continue to practice the presence of God—not in a great leap but in small steps of the possible. Let us do little things for God, a small remembrance, one inward act of worship. The value of an action lies not in its size but in its motive—love for God.

Those who have the gale of the Holy Spirit go forward even in sleep. If the vessel of our soul is still tossed with winds and storms, let us wake the Lord who reposes in it, and he will quickly calm the sea. (p. 45)

In his life and work at the monastery, Brother Lawrence tears down the unbiblical wall between sacred and secular. The practice of the presence of God in prayer and work makes every activity holy— dedicated to his service. Just as Jean-Pierre de Caussade empha- sizes the "sacrament of the present moment," so Brother Lawrence stresses the "sacredness of the present task." They are two sides of the same coin.

In his last published letter, dated February 6, 1691, Brother Lawrence wrote:

Let all our business be to *know* God; the more one *knows* him, the more one *desires* to know him . . . the deeper and more extensive our *knowledge,* the greater will be our *love.* . . . I hope from his mercy the favor to see him within a few days. Let us pray for one another. (pp. 46-47)

Brother Lawrence took to his bed two days later and died within the week.

The Blessed Hope

Life is a one-way street. No matter how many detours we may take, none of them ever leads back. So we must learn to do the best we can right now with who we are and what we have.

When we grasp the importance of the present, we learn to prize the "now" of our existence. We then say with the psalmist, "This is the day the LORD has made; let us rejoice and be glad in it" (Ps 118:24).

We do so, however, in light of our future. "We have to live one day at a time, but in the one day we are living for eternity" (anon). The apostle Paul links the present with the future in a command and a promise:

> Live self-controlled, upright and godly lives in this present age, while we wait for the blessed hope—the glorious appearing of our great God and Savior, Jesus Christ, who gave himself for us to redeem us . . . a people that are his very own, eager to do what is good. (Tit 2:12-14)

* * *

Questions for Reflection and Discussion

1. To what extent are you living in the past or future in some area of your life?

2. What impresses you about de Caussade's view of the "present moment" lived in commitment to the will of God?

3. How can you learn from Brother Lawrence's "practice of the presence of God" in the ordinary tasks you face today?

4. What does the "blessed hope" of Christ's return mean to you today?

Epilogue:
The Tapestry

*T*he following is a final reflection from Jean-Pierre de Caussade (from *Abandonment to Divine Providence,* p. 104).

The Tapestry

As God and the believer work together, God's achievement is like the front of a lovely tapestry. The worker employed on such a tapestry sees only the back as he adds stitch after stitch with his needle. Yet all these stitches are slowly creating a magnificent picture which happens in all its glory only when every stitch is done and it is viewed from the right side. But all this beauty cannot be seen as it is being created.

It is the same with the self-abandoned believer, who sees only God and his duty. To fulfill this duty moment by moment consists in adding tiny stitches to the work. Yet it is by these stitches that

God accomplishes those marvels of which we sometimes catch a glimpse now, but which will not be truly known until the great day of eternity.

How good and wise are the ways of God! All that is sublime and exalted, great and admirable in the task of achieving holiness and perfection, he has kept for his own power. But everything that is small, simple and easy he leaves us to tackle with the help of grace.

Appendix 1

Hearing the Word of God

Christ is the Word of God who became flesh for us.
Through the discipline of the Book, the Word of God can
continue to become flesh in us. Read the Scriptures as
God's most intimate word for us.
HENRI NOUWEN

*I*n our hectic lives, many of us sense the need to listen to God. But busy schedules often keep us from even making the effort. We may say, "After I graduate and get away from all these textbooks . . ." or "Once the kids are older and need less attention . . ." But we need to learn *now* to be quiet before God—to hear his voice through Scripture and as we pray. Once we do this, much of life's tyranny will relax its grip. We may even begin to understand these ancient words about Bible study:

Oh, how I love your law!

I meditate on it all day long. . . .

Seven times a day I praise you

for your righteous laws.

Great peace have they who love your law,

and nothing can make them stumble.

(Ps 119:97, 164-65)

Following are some basic helps for studying the Bible, alone or with others, to help you hear God as he speaks through holy Scripture. Appendix two will help you learn more about praying on the basis of what you read.

We are not likely to make the time for serious Bible study unless we are convinced of its importance. Life's pressures and demands already claim all our waking hours. So what priority should we give to studying these ancient documents?

Meaning for our lives must be found in the purpose of the Creator who has given life to us and will hold us accountable for the way we use it. Fortunately, we are not left to speculate what that purpose may be. God has taken the initiative to reveal himself and the relationship he desires to have with us. "In the past God spoke to our forefathers through the prophets at many times and in various ways" (Heb 1:1). God spoke though mighty acts of judgment and mercy throughout history, and he also spoke through his messengers who proclaimed the meaning of those acts. The written records, which became the Old and New Testaments, have long been cherished, studied and obeyed by God's people, and they provide our most reliable authority for living. As the psalmist declared, "Your word is a lamp to my feet and a light for my path" (Ps 119:105).

The Word of God in Human Words
Part of what is recorded for us in the Bible is the true story of how God spoke a *living* word. The writer to the Hebrews continues, "But in these last days he has spoken to us by his Son, whom he appointed heir of all things, and through whom he made the universe" (Heb 1:2). And the apostle John explains in classic words, "In the beginning was the Word, and the Word was with God, and the Word was God. . . . The Word became flesh and made his dwelling among us" (Jn 1:1, 14). In Jesus Christ the act of God and the word of God are one; both the saving actions and the revealing words that we need are found in him.

In order to understand the Scriptures, we need to appreciate the distinctive roles of *revelation, inspiration* and *interpretation.*

1. Revelation from God. In the Bible it is God himself who takes the initiative—unlike other religions, which feature the human search for God. All that we know of God is a gracious gift of his self-revelation. It has come through widely diverse personalities, cultures and forms of literature. But always the message was *received* by the prophets and others who wrote it down; they did not claim to originate it.

The apostle Peter makes this point clear: "No prophecy in Scripture ever came from the prophets themselves. . . . It was the Holy Spirit who moved the prophets to speak from God" (2 Pet 1:20-21 NLT). The movement is downward: from God to his people. A typical example is found in Micah 1:1: "The word of the LORD that came to Micah of Moresheth."

One of the greatest intellectuals of the Western world, the apostle Paul, declared that his teaching came from God: "This is what we speak, not in words taught us by human wisdom but in words taught by the Spirit, expressing spiritual truths in spiritual words" (1 Cor 2:13). Although Paul's keen mind was involved in his teaching and writing, his authority was not based on his own insight and wisdom.

Revelation is the process by which God chooses his prophets, works in their lives and reveals a message to be proclaimed to his people. Although the prophecy sometimes foretells the future, it usually aims at religious heresy and social and economic evils, calling for a return to the true God and the elimination of injustice.

2. Inspired writings. As valuable as those prophecies were at the time, they could have little benefit for following generations unless preserved in written form. While we often speak of the *prophets* as inspired, in reality it was their *writings* that were inspired. Paul teaches this important principle in a classic statement to his young protégé Timothy.

But as for you, continue in what you have learned and firmly believed, knowing from whom you learned it, and how from childhood you have known the sacred writings that are able to instruct you for salvation through faith in Christ Jesus. All Scripture is inspired by God and is useful for teaching, for reproof, for correction, and for training in righteousness, so that everyone who belongs to God may be proficient, equipped for every good work (2 Tim 3:14-17 NRSV).

As usual in Paul's writings, doctrinal teaching addresses the needs of a specific situation. The truth of Scripture is not given simply to fill our minds; its ultimate purpose is to shape our lives. A prime purpose of the "sacred writings" is to instruct us for salvation. They tell the good news of Christ's life, death and resurrection. They train us in right living so that we may be equipped for good works.

We also learn that all Scripture is inspired (literally "expired") by God; in other words it is "God-breathed." Note that Paul describes the "sacred writings" as inspired, not the authors. This corresponds with the 1 Corinthians 2:13 statement that his teaching is in "words taught by the Spirit."

Some say they believe the authors were inspired but not their words. On that basis, however, we could not have confidence in biblical teachings, since it is the words that communicate their ideas.

By analogy, we would not think of saying, "Beethoven is an inspired musician, but I can't go along with all of his notes." Or, "I accept the truth of Einstein's relativity theory but not all of his numbers." No, just as the composer's notes comprise the music and the scientist's numbers define the theory, so the biblical words communicate the author's message.

Many reject "verbal" inspiration because they think it means mechanical dictation. Not so. The biblical authors display their individual culture, language, personality and experience. We are not told *how* the Holy Spirit inspired the sacred writings—only that they reliably convey the divine message free from teaching what is false. For that reason we can accept the Bible as entirely trustworthy and our final authority in matters of faith and conduct.

Through our study of Scripture we come to know God the Creator and Redeemer as our Lord and Savior. We discover the moral and spiritual laws built into the fabric of human nature. And we find the direction we need to give our lives meaning and purpose in the service of our Lord Jesus Christ.

3. Interpreting the Bible. Many steer away from studying the Bible because they believe it is too difficult to understand without formal theological education. Others are put off when they see people interpreting the Bible to confirm their own ideas.

Are you in one of these two categories? If so, take heart. The following basic principles of interpretation can help you avoid both extremes as you study a passage of Scripture.

First, identify the *kind of literature.* The Bible is more than a book; it is a veritable library of sixty-six "books." And it has many different kinds of literature: prose and poetry, historical narratives and parables, biographies, proverbs, letters, sermons and prophecies. Deciding what kind you are studying is half the battle. For example, a parable is not a historical account but a story with a spiritual truth. A letter often reveals the circumstances of the church or individual addressed.

Second, determine the *meaning of the text.* At the time of the Reformation many biblical interpreters indulged in fanciful allegories to amaze and delight their hearers.

> *Look for the "plain meaning" of the words.*

Often their imagination ran wild as they spiritualized a passage. So Martin Luther insisted on discovering the "plain meaning" of the text. In other words, look for a message that could be understood by ordinary readers—both then and now!

If a proposed interpretation would not have been understood at the time of writing, it should not be taken as the biblical author's meaning.

We also need to keep in mind that a word can have more than one meaning. For example, take our word *bar* and think of its various meanings—from a piece of soap to the practice of law. With such different connotations we might wonder how to determine which one is used by the author. The answer is simple: the meaning is always determined by the *context* and *usage*. In other words, what subject is the writer dealing with? How is the word used in this setting? This principle guards against the danger of a "word study" that lifts all the biblical occurrences out of their context and arbitrarily assigns them a single meaning derived from a particular author.

Translations of the Bible

Despite their differences, the New Testament books have one basic characteristic in common. They are all written in a form of Greek that is significantly different from the classical language of 350 to 300 B.C. used by the great philosophers, dramatists and historians. When this fact was discovered, long ago, scholars concluded, out of reverence for the Word of God, that the New Testament had been written in a special "Holy Ghost" Greek given expressly for that sacred purpose.

In the last century, however, archaeological discoveries of letters, civil documents and business transactions have showed that the Greek of the New Testament was the Koine, a dialect that had become the everyday language of the Hellenistic world. What a blow! But as Bible scholars recovered from the shock they began to appreciate that when God communicated his message he chose a language that everyone could understand. *The Word of God was given in fully human words.*

At the end of the fourth century Jerome produced a Latin edition of the Bible in the common speech of the ancient Romans. For a thousand years this translation was the widely accepted text throughout Western Europe. In the sixteenth century William Tyndale, an English religious reformer, produced a version of the New Testament that became a basis for the King James Bible of 1611. A century earlier Martin Luther produced a popular German translation of the Bible that has also been widely read until the present time.

Our century has witnessed a variety of translations both popular and scholarly. In the 1940s English scholar J. B. Phillips produced the very readable *Letters to Young Churches;* it captured the attention of thousands who had never before opened a Bible. Soon Kenneth Taylor published The Living Bible, whose vivid, modern English often runs to a paraphrase.

Meanwhile two scholarly committees worked on major translations for general reading and study. The Revised Standard Version made its appearance in 1952; the New International Version was published in 1985. Both represent the never-ending process of making the Bible available in the form of English most widely current in our day. Further steps were taken with the production of the New Revised Standard Version in 1989 and the New Living Translation in 1996.

While it is wonderful to have the Word of God in easily understood English, we may well ask whether the many translations and study Bibles are really producing a clearer understanding and stronger application of holy Scripture. We should avoid being simply "version hoppers" who jump from one text to another to compare and criticize, rather than staying with one version long enough for solid study.

Truth in Action

Have you ever been asked, "Do you take the Bible literally?" How do you answer that question?

Since it calls for more than a simple yes or no answer, I usually reply, "I take the literal parts literally and the figurative parts figuratively." That leads directly to the question of what the word *literal* means. Usually the person is asking, "Do you believe that the biblical records are true? Did the reported events really happen?"

Discussion of this issue is often muddied by a basic literary misunderstanding. It is wrongly assumed that *literal* means fact, while *figurative* means fancy (or myth). Like any great literature, the Bible employs many figures of speech to catch the eye and stir the imagination. This figurative language, however, is often used to communicate facts. On the other hand, a fairy story or myth could be told with the use of only literal statements, but that would not make it factual. (And it would certainly make the story less satisfying to the reader.)

So the fundamental question is this: "What does the author intend to communicate?" For example, what does King David mean when he reports, "The strong arm of the Lord saved me from my enemies"? Since the Israelites were commanded not to make any carved image for worship, this is obviously figurative language; God doesn't really have an arm. David's use of this metaphor is more effective than saying, "The Lord helped me dodge the spears and arrows to escape being killed."

The psalms especially are full of anthropomorphisms that represent God as a person. The truth about God is revealed in his actions. Yet many critics consider it crude to picture God as loving, hating, shouting, remembering, forgetting. They prefer the lofty Greek ideas of God as the Good, the Noble, the Beautiful, the True. To this there are two replies.

First, if the infinite God who is Spirit desires to reveal himself to his people, what better way is there than to use categories of human thought and action? These figures of speech graphically reveal God as intensely personal in his concern for our lives. This language can be understood around the world in all cultures.

Second, we cannot love and be loved by an idea, a concept of the Good and Beautiful. While the biblical human terms may alienate a critical scholar, they are a great comfort to those who desire a personal relationship with the living God. At the same time we realize that he is far greater in many dimensions we cannot grasp. But in the words of C. S. Lewis, "We can be confident that God is at least personal."

Three Key Questions

Three keys unlock the treasures of the Bible in our daily life.

1. What does it say? This question first searches for the facts of the passage. Unfortunately, many discussions of the Bible jump into interpretation without adequate attention to the facts. Familiarity with the Bible can be a disadvantage here: we may tend to "know" what it says even before reading it. *Observation* of the text asks factual questions of who, what, when, where.

A mature Christian who had read through the Bible each year for the last decade told me that he had tried something different this year. Using an unfamiliar modern translation, he decided to read the Gospels as if he had never seen them before, observing the facts closely. He was amazed at what he saw for the first time in chapters that he had read since childhood.

2. What does it mean? At this point in our study we deal with *interpretation* of the facts. For example, Mark tells us of a certain leper who came to Jesus pleading for healing. "Moved with pity, Jesus stretched out his hand and touched him" (Mk 1:41, NRSV). We now ask questions of meaning: Why? How? What was the significance of this action? Why did Jesus touch him? What do you think it meant to the leper?

Usually the answers to these questions of interpretation come from the passage itself. Occasionally we need to turn to another part of the Bible or to a commentary for additional information. But it is surprising how much we can gain from our own reading and meditation. So let us not turn too quickly for outside help. After all, the biblical author expected his readers, who had no commentaries, to follow the train of thought and get his message.

> *What does it say?*
> *What does it mean?*
> *What does it mean*
> *to me?*

3. What does this truth mean to me today? Often neglected, this question of application is essential to fulfill the purpose of our Bible study. Without a vital connection between truth and action, our study remains on cloud eleven in the realm of ideas.

As we take time day by day to discover God's message for us, we increasingly see life from his perspective. New light shines on our opportunities and difficulties. We find ourselves able to say, along with the psalmist, "Your word is a lamp to my feet and a light for my path" (Ps 119:105). But more than that, we have a renewed sense of God's presence as we go into the day to make our lives count for his purposes in the church and the world.

Bible Discovery Groups

In recent years small Bible study groups have flourished throughout the country. New translations in modern English motivate many people—both Christians and seekers—to find out more about what the Bible teaches. These groups assume several different shapes.

Many have no designated leader; the members share their insights as they read and discuss the passage. Other groups look to teachers who expound the Scripture, directly communicating what they have learned. Each method has its strength and weakness.

The first offers ample opportunity for the members to share their discoveries. But a lack of leadership permits the discussion to stray from the passage and get bogged down in irrelevant issues. Groups with a teacher can avoid this problem, but at the cost of remaining dependent on that person to explain the biblical message.

Between those extremes is the Bible Discovery Group, which has a leader who starts the discussion and keeps it moving through the selected Scripture. The leader is not a teacher in the sense of telling the others what the text means. Rather this person asks questions that enable the members to discover the truths for themselves.

When participants get involved in a Bible Discovery Group that applies basic principles of interpretation, they are surprised with the results. Both of the common fears—that the Bible is too difficult for the average reader and that it supports any interpretation someone wants—dissipate in the give and take of open discussion of the text.

A second benefit of discovery groups is the opportunity for members to interact with the Bible at the point of their individual need. Sometimes it is asked, "If there is no teacher, won't the group miss some truths in the passage?" The answer is twofold: "Intellectually, yes; practically, no."

The purpose of the study is not to get all the truths at one sitting. Our aim is to *grasp the main teachings and put at least one into practice.* If we are candid we will admit that our greatest lack is not intellectual but practical. One truth people discover for themselves is worth many that someone else tells them. Applied by the Holy Spirit, that teaching achieves the goal of Bible study for that session.

A third advantage of this method is that the leader doesn't have to be a scholar who knows all the answers. Actually, a new Christian with relatively little knowledge of Scripture can become an effective discussion leader. The group concentrates on one chapter at a time as it moves through a book of the Bible. Since the discussion doesn't jump around the Bible as in a topical study, the leader need not be familiar with everything from Genesis to Revelation.

A commitment to stay with the passage makes an even playing field for all the members. It means that someone who has never read the Bible is not at a disadvantage sitting beside another who has a seminary degree. In fact, the former may make a more positive contribution to a discussion free from an importation of theological problems.

There are further advantages in a discovery group. Since few people can answer questions while thinking about something else, the leader knows whether the members are paying attention. Their answers also show the extent to which the passage is being understood. Open discussion encourages an expression of different views as the members interact with each other. Sharing of how the truths apply to individual lives proves to be an encouragement.

Leading the Discussion

Following are the steps involved in conducting the discussion.

1. Choose a convenient place and time; start and end promptly.

Arrange the chairs in a circle and have extra Bibles available—all the same version, if possible.

2. Start with prayer. If we really believe the Holy Spirit is our Teacher, we unitedly ask him for help.

3. Take time to go through the passage as a group. Don't assume it has been read ahead of time. Get volunteers to read aloud, paragraph by paragraph. For a long chapter have the group read silently with a thought question in mind. This can be followed by a short "popcorn" idea session with brief sharing of initial impressions—but no discussion at this point!

4. Never, never, never answer your own questions. Give the group time to find the answers. If the silence is too long, rephrase your question. Do not always be satisfied with the first answer or fill in the rest yourself. You can ask, "Does anyone want to add anything?" If an answer seems wrong ask, "What do the rest of you think?" Remember that you are not the authority; soon correction begins to come from the members. If someone asks you a question, toss it back to the group.

5. As the leader be prepared to step in, summarize and move on with another question. Keep to the passage at hand. If someone makes irrelevant comments or imports ideas from another part of the Bible, ask, "Where in the text do you find that?"

6. Be grateful for every answer. Appreciate each person who contributes even though the comment may be only partly right. Encourage rather than bluntly correct. Be prepared to learn from the group.

7. Watch the time. Keep the discussion moving, yet allow time for various applications to be made. You may want to skip some questions that don't fit in as the study progresses. Mark "optional" questions that can be dropped if time is getting short, to make sure the most important points are included.

8. Be sure to end at the appointed time, since busy people need to plan their schedules. However, you can offer to stay on for those who want additional discussion.

The foregoing principles and practice of Bible study and group discussion have been time-tested in many kinds of situations. Yet we must recognize that technique is not the final word. If we meet God in our own study and are excited about what he has taught us, this reality will get across even if our methods are not perfect.

*   *   *

Questions for Reflection and Discussion

1. In what way has God been revealing himself to you recently?

2. How have the Scriptures been equipping you for Christian life and service? List certain passages that have been meaningful lately.

3. What principles of biblical interpretation do you find most helpful?

4. Can you think of several friends who might enjoy participating in a Bible Discovery Group?

Appendix 2

Praying the Scriptures

The decisive preparation for prayer
lies not in the prayer itself, but in the life
prior to the prayer. The distractions and dryness
in our prayer spring largely from our faulty dispositions,
doings and driftings when out of prayer.
FRIEDRICH VON HÜGEL

*H*ow often our prayer life is plagued with fatigue and wandering thought. We feel too tired to persist. The harder we try to concentrate, the more other thoughts crowd in. It seems somewhat like being told, "Don't think about a hippopotamus for the next five minutes."

The cause and cure for these distractions is often located some hours or days before the prayer itself. The fast pace and urgent pressures of our lives take their toll, sapping the energy needed to pray. So preparation for a morning quiet time may have to begin several nights beforehand by going to bed a half-hour earlier. Or scanning a list of the day's activities may pinpoint the need to eliminate a task, or at least shorten one, to foster an atmosphere of peace for the coming prayer time.

Another aid in getting our prayer life off the ground is making the Bible's prayers our own. A primary source is the psalms, which contain all the major forms of prayer. Four of these forms are easily remembered in the acronym ACTS: adoration, confession, thanksgiving, supplication.

Starting our quiet time each day with a psalm has two advantages. First, it helps us focus outside ourselves, on the experience of the psalm writer. We travel with him as he expresses a dimension of life in his own words. When we come to the end of the psalm, we can continue to pray on that theme in words of our own. Second, as we start our devotions by listening to the Word in this way, we allow God to open the conversation on the subject of his choice.

ACTS: Adoration, Confession, Thanksgiving, Supplication

Following are brief excerpts from psalms that illustrate these themes.

1. Adoration. This kind of prayer is an act of worship—reverent love and ardent devotion. It is praise and glory with a focus on who God is in himself, his power and love. He is the Maker of heaven and earth, the Lord and Judge of history, the Shepherd of his covenant people.

Psalm 100 proclaims his majesty and compassion.

Shout for joy to the LORD, all the earth.
     Worship the LORD with gladness;
     come before him with joyful songs.
Know that the LORD is God.
     It is he who made us, and we are his;
     we are his people, the sheep of his pasture. (vv. 1-3)

Psalm 145 simply delights in God's greatness.

     I will exalt you, my God the King;
     I will praise your name for ever and ever.
Every day I will praise you
     and extol your name for ever and ever.
Great is the LORD and most worthy of praise;
     his greatness no one can fathom. (vv. 1-3)

2. Confession of sin. King David was described as "a man after God's own heart." Yet, as we have noted, he committed adultery and murder. While other kings perpetrated worse crimes with no conscience, the Jewish monarch poured out his repentance in Psalm 51.

Have mercy on me, O God,
    according to your unfailing love;
according to your great compassion
    blot out my transgressions.
Wash away all my iniquity
    and cleanse me from my sin.
For I know my transgressions,
    and my sin is always before me. . . .
Hide your face from my sins
    and blot out all my iniquity.
Create in me a pure heart, O God,
    and renew a steadfast spirit within me.
Do not cast me from your presence
    or take your Holy Spirit from me. (vv. 1-3, 9-10)

As you read this prayer, the Holy Spirit may bring to mind some sin of your own—less violent but still significant—calling for repentance.

3. Thanksgiving. While adoration focuses on God himself, thanksgiving praises God for what he has done for us. Following are the opening four verses of Psalm 103, which marvelously combine the two themes.

Praise the LORD, O my soul;
    all my inmost being, praise his holy name.
Praise the LORD, O my soul,
    and forget not all his benefits—
who forgives all your sins
    and heals all your diseases,
who redeems your life from the pit
    and crowns you with love and compassion,

who satisfies your desires with good things
    so that your youth is renewed like the eagle's.
The LORD works righteousness
    and justice for all the oppressed. (vv. 1-6)

Psalm 30 is also a psalm of thanksgiving—a witness to God's deliverance from a variety of difficulties and appreciation for health.

I will exalt you, O LORD,
    for you lifted me out of the depths
    and did not let my enemies gloat over me.
O LORD my God, I called to you for help
    and you healed me. . . .
You turned my wailing into dancing;
    you removed my sackcloth and clothed me with joy,
that my heart may sing to you and not be silent.
    O LORD my God, I will give you thanks forever. (vv. 1-2, 11-12)

You may find you can use these psalms to identify and express your gratitude to God for various blessings and benefits he has given you.

4. Supplication. What about our own personal needs and those of others? What about our stress levels and deadlines? The word *supplication,* though not widely used today, is significant. It is a humble, earnest entreaty. This kind of reverent, fervent prayer brings our request to God for his gracious response. This the psalms do frequently and with vigor. You may find encouragement in the example of David in Psalm 5.

Give ear to my words, O LORD,
    consider my sighing.
Listen to my cry for help,
    my King and my God,
    for to you I pray.
In the morning . . .
    I lay my requests before you
    and wait in expectation. (vv. 1-3)

Try going through the psalms, one a day. As you allow God to open the conversation on a subject of his choice, you can respond in the appropriate way.

Discussion of prayer sooner or later turns to the question of answers. Supplication or petition asks God to do something for someone—ourselves or others. We may need healing of an illness, guidance for a decision, money for bills. We wonder when, how or even *if* there will be an answer—a provision for the need.

These concerns, valid as they may be, find a different focus in a statement of Henry Hardy (1869-1946), better known as "Father Andrew." He declares,

> The great answer to prayer is the power to pray more. We have not so much to think whether prayers are answered as whether prayer answers. . . . God could give us no greater gift than the power of perseverance in prayer. (*Christ the Companion,* privately printed, 1996, p. 1.)

*   *   *

Questions for Reflection and Discussion

1. What is the chief benefit of praying the psalms? Consider using those quoted here as a basis for your prayer during this next week.

2. What light does Father Andrew's statement throw on the way you have been seeking answers to your prayers?

3. In what way can you put the ACTS formula to use?

Appendix 3

At Your Leisure

Where is the life we have lost in living?
Where is the wisdom we have lost in knowledge?
Where is the knowledge we have lost in information?
T. S. ELIOT

*W*hen someone recommends a book to read or a film to see "at your leisure," how do you react? *Leisure? Whatever would that be?*

In one respect the term *leisure* is like the elephant in Aesop's Fables. One day three blind men day encountered this strange creature on the outskirts of town. They carefully explored it with their hands and then returned to report their discovery. The first, who had touched a tusk, said, "An elephant is hard and smooth like porcelain." The second had felt the skin and declared, "No, it is rough, like untanned leather." The third man, who had grasped the tail, objected, "The creature is more like a heavy rope."

So it is with leisure; our perception depends on our experience. As with time, no one definition fits all cases.

Yet the different definitions have one thing in common; their meaning is related primarily to our work: "time off," "free time," "spare time," "vacation." The dictionary emphasizes that aspect, defining leisure as "freedom from time-consuming duties, respon-sibilities, or activities . . . at one's convenience." Note that the definition is basically negative: "freedom from" certain duties or responsibilities to which we are committed.

Those definitions, however, leave open the crucial question: freedom *for* what? True freedom is understood in terms of its purpose and use. It is not simply independence from limitations. Likewise, *the meaning of leisure lies in its purpose.*

First, we note that the Bible has no word for our concept of "leisure." The Greek word *eukaireō* (which occurs once, in Mk 6:31) means "to have a favorable opportunity" to do something. It is translated "chance" in the NIV. However, biblical writers have much to say about "rest." The Genesis 1 creation narrative pictures God as a workman who accomplishes his daily tasks for six days, then *rests* on the seventh, satisfied that everything he has created is very good.

This model of Israel's work was made the basis of the fourth commandment in Exodus 20:8-11. "Remember the Sabbath day by keeping it holy. . . . On it you shall not do any work. . . . the LORD . . . rested on the seventh day." The sabbath was also a reminder to the Israelites of their deliverance from bondage in Egypt (Deut 5:15). And it showed that their life had an element of "free" time, not just *from* work but also *for* celebrations and festivals—*kairos* occasions and events.

Unfortunately, in New Testament times the day's restful charac-ter was obscured by legalism. Many detailed laws prescribed what minimal necessary activities could be performed. Ironically, ensur-ing that no work was done on the Sabbath became very hard work! And it was another sort of bondage.

In the early church the principle of weekly gatherings for wor-ship was continued, although the Jewish sabbath (Saturday) was replaced by the first day of the week (Sunday). Old Testament liturgical services gave way to less structured forms. Other days were also reserved for religious services (Col 2:16). As the church spread, various cultural forms enhanced its worship.

We have seen how the industrial revolution in the West has regulated work and much of life by the clock. The practice of a scheduled vacation, free from work, is based on the linear view of time as a measurable period. But a genuine appreciation of leisure goes beyond that view to another dimension denoted by the popular term "quality time."

This is a timely event or opportunity, a special occasion that calls for decision or action—or enjoyment. Here the emphasis is on the quality rather than the quantity of time involved, the value rather than the length.

Genuine Recreation

Like Aesop's elephant, modern leisure has a variety of shapes. In leisure there is more than rest to recharge our physical and emotional batteries. Leisure is basically "recreation," not in the popular sense of play—fun and games—but in the original meaning to "re-create." Genuine leisure offers an element of personal fulfillment.

It has been said that whereas work is something you do for others, *leisure is done for yourself.* Although an oversimplification, this statement focuses on an essential difference. When you work for someone else you have a "job description" with targets and schedules that prescribe expected performance. If you are self-employed you still have an obligation to produce. Even if your "work" consists of family responsibilities, you are required to "perform" the tasks needed by those who are dependent on you.

On the other hand, you choose a leisure activity to meet your own need for genuine "re-creation." This principle should be applied not only to your initial selection but also to the process of doing it. Otherwise from force of habit you may drift into a timetable that generates pressure to produce results. In doing so you will lose the primary value of your leisure: to become more of a *total* person. One couple, trying to learn relaxation in the midst of an intense life pattern, bought the board game Life and began to play. They approached it so seriously and competitively that they soon stopped, exhausted! For them, leisure had to come in other forms.

For many of us, increasing pressures squeeze the amount of time we spend on leisure. Yet the basic problem is not a shortage of time but our attitude and the ordering of priorities. The terms "free time" and "spare time" show that we evaluate leisure in relationship to work rather than what it offers in itself. We need to overcome the view that leisure is primarily something that enhances our work.

An adequate period of genuine leisure affords a break from the daily rhythms of our life. We can see more clearly what important dimensions of life are being neglected or impoverished. We discover an opportunity to reflect on who we are, where we have been and where we are going as persons.

How to Create and Use Leisure Time

We need to give leisure the importance it deserves by scheduling the necessary blocks of time. On a monthly calendar page, color in some blocks that you will reserve for "rest and recreation"—then guard them with your life. (See figure 4.) *There is no "quality" time without adequate "quantity."* The periods may be as short as an hour or as long as a week or two, depending on the circumstances. But leisure must have a high priority that resists the inevitable encroachment of the urgent, squeezing out what doesn't seem so important at the moment. You may be in a temporary crisis period that simply does not allow any time for leisure; if so, plan ahead for a time when you *can* take a break. Just looking forward to that time may relieve your present pressure a bit.

> *"I'm so busy I can't afford to take time for leisure."*
> *No, you're so busy you can't afford **not** to take time for leisure.*

The practice of leisure calls for a balance between our needs and available resources. We need to ask: "What kinds of activity will bring me satisfaction, drawing on abilities not already harnessed by my work? Which of them are within the range of my resources?" The

Monthly Calendar

Figure 4.   Blocks of Time Set Aside for Leisure.

answers will be as different as the questioners.

Select your activities with care. Avoid the temptation to plan a tight schedule that adds its own deadlines to ones you already have. Your activities should go beyond simple compensation for what is missing in your work, although they may well have an element of this result. Avoid doing what you think you *should* be doing during a leisure time slot; do whatever personally delights and refreshes you.

Several major categories of recreation do not require a large amount of time or money. God's creation affords a wide variety of opportunities. Depending on where you live, you can drive through a woods, walk along a beach, or even sit on a sunny bench in a city park enjoying the leaves, the birds and the sky.

Fulfillment can also be experienced through developing creative gifts that do not depend on climate or calendar. It may be learning to play a musical instrument; composing songs or poems; working with wood, stained glass or pottery; growing flowers; photography, painting or anything else that you enjoy. Many kinds of hobbies—depending on your temperament—offer an opportunity to refresh yourself and gain a new dimension of personal satisfaction through creativity.

Leisure can also afford an opportunity to strengthen relationships with family and friends—time that goes beyond present superficial encounters. It may involve doing together some of the above activities. It may involve just sitting around and talking for several hours, a luxury you don't usually allow yourself.

An arch enemy of leisure, as well as of our daily devotions, is the modern cult of busyness. Society encourages us to define ourselves in terms of our *possessions* and our *reputation.* The pursuit of both can keep us busy for all our waking hours, spurred by an activism that is never satisfied.

Leisure offers a unique opportunity to place greater emphasis on *making a life, not just a living*. It enables us to "stop, look and listen" to the question of who we are and what is most important to us. It should not be a time to evaluate work goals but to explore other dimensions of our life, to think in terms of our total person. It is an occasion to bring our life into better balance as we manage it under the lordship of Jesus Christ.

*   *   *

Questions for Reflection and Discussion

1. In terms of your own life, how have you been looking at leisure?

2. What activities of "genuine recreation" would you most like to pursue?

3. List three ways (even if small ones) in which you can create and use leisure time in your life right now.

Appendix 4

It's About Time

*There is a time for everything, and a season for every
activity under heaven: a time to be born and a time to die,
a time to plant and a time to uproot . . . a time to weep and
a time to laugh, a time to mourn and a time to dance . . . a
time to be silent and a time to speak.*
ECCLESIASTES

What is time? The striking of a town clock? The urgent
10 . . . 9 . . . 8 . . . 7 . . . of a space shuttle countdown? Spring
and autumn? The wrinkled face of an old man on a park bench?
No, those are only measures of time, signs of its passage; they
are not time itself.

Time: Problem, Tyrant or Friend?
Time's nature eludes us. Like the wind, which we also cannot see,
time is known by its effects. Philosophers try to define it, some with
mathematical formulas, then clash over their interpretations. No
wonder! A dictionary devotes more than half a column to about
thirty different definitions of *time.*

In daily life we use the word in a wide variety of ways. As a
measurable *commodity,* time is treated like something to be found
or made, gained or lost, saved or wasted, used wisely or foolishly.

We say, "She has too much time on her hands," "I've spent hours on this project," "He took up my whole morning, and I got nothing done!"

Time is also viewed as an *opportunity* or *special occasion:* a timely event or time out, ripe for decision or action. It can be an *experience:* either good ("I had the time of my life") or bad ("They really gave me a hard time"). Time is sometimes pictured as an *action:* it can drag, march or fly.

This variety of meanings shows us how misguided and futile it is to look for a single definition of time that fits all situations. As with other words in daily language, a specific meaning is determined by its context and usage. What is the author writing or talking about, and how is the term used?

Most talk about time today rings with a note of frustration and urgency.

"I'll try to find time."

"I just ran out of time."

"Where does the time go?"

Ironically, although our modern technology produces many labor-saving devices, time seems ever more scarce.

Here we will briefly look at several uses of time. But rather than try to *define its essence,* we will *describe some of its effects.* On this point we take a clue from St. Augustine (A.D. 354-430), one of the greatest Western scholars and a devout, practical Christian.

For what is Time? Who is able easily and briefly to explain it? And yet in our usual discourse what do we more familiarly and knowingly mention than Time? And surely we understand it well enough when we speak of it; we also understand it when in conversation we hear it named. What, then, is Time? If nobody asks me I know; but if I desired to explain it to someone who should ask me, I simply do not know.

In other words, we can use what something *does* even when we do not understand what it *is*—like electricity and gravitation, for example. Likewise we can state something about what it *is not.*

Cultural Views

We have noted a basic difference between American and Mexican or Filipino views of time and their effects on daily life. They can be further summarized and contrasted as follows.

Future-oriented cultures live and work by the clock. They set goals, plan how to reach them, decide on schedules and act accordingly. The future belongs to those who plan for it! Time is viewed and valued as a precious resource—limited and always running out. People in this kind of culture

☐ set appropriate time periods for accomplishing tasks.

☐ select goals and prepare detailed plans to reach them.

☐ plan a meeting carefully to accomplish as much as possible in the amount of time scheduled for it.

☐ are sensitive about punctuality for the beginning and end of an allotted time.

Event-oriented cultures, on the other hand, focus on the importance of the moment and the feeling of completeness in the experience. Those people are primarily interested in who is present, what is going on and how the event can be enhanced. They

☐ are not too concerned with time periods.

☐ bring people together, without a detailed schedule, to see what will happen.

☐ work through a problem or idea regardless of time.

☐ live in the present without a detailed schedule for the future.

In practice, however, these two views are usually both present in varying degrees, often more as an emphasis or tendency than as an absolute. Within a given society there can be various combinations in different ethnic subcultures and in the lives of individuals. To whatever degree this distinction exists, it is important in human relationships.

In recent decades, discussion of time has emphasized another distinction, the importance of two opposite meanings: *external* time, measured by the clock (and the same for all), and *internal* time, indicated by personal experience and feelings. Following are terms used to describe this difference:

external	internal
outer	inner
objective	subjective
measured	lived

The meaning of these terms is determined by their context and usage. For example, two Minnesota friends go to Bermuda for a winter week of vacation. Most of the days turn out to be cloudy and misty. Upon returning home, they both give the same "outer-time" report of travel and accommodations. Yet their "inner-time" reports are radically different. The one who loved golf had a wonderful time, because the green wasn't covered with snow and the days weren't hot and sticky. On the other hand, the other, who loved sunbathing, had a terrible week, because the only sunny skies were in the travel brochure.

Measured time was the same for both: one week. *Lived time* flew for the golfer but dragged for the sunbather. Each person's inner time is different from the steady pace of the clock, depending on what is happening around and within us.

Time and Motion

Our colorful metaphors that picture time doing all sorts of things cloud the basic fact that time itself does nothing. Rather it is simply *a measure of motion and change throughout the natural world.* For example, the day is the measure for the earth's rotation on its axis; the year for its revolution around the sun; the month for the moon's revolution around the earth. At the other end of the speed scale, the light-year is a measure of the distance light travels in a year.

For a parallel, imagine a mountain stream flowing through your property in the country. Day and night the water steadily makes its way toward the sea. First consider what you cannot do to it. You cannot hurry, slow, stop or reverse its flow. Nor can you increase or decrease the amount of water. What, then, can you do with this stream? You can wash your clothes, fish, swim or install a paddle wheel to generate electricity.

Now suppose the stream is about fifty feet wide. As the owner you decide to use it to generate your electricity. So you install five paddle wheels across the stream from shore to shore. Your expectations for full productivity run high. But to your disappointment, only the wheels toward the middle of the stream turn at the predicted speed. Those near the shore in shallow water rotate more slowly. What is the problem? Too little water? No; your planning was faulty in assuming that all the paddle wheels would be equally productive.

Like most parables, this story teaches one important lesson. The flow of water is similar to other kinds of motion and change measured by the passage of time. Neither the water nor time itself, however, determines how it is to be used. Less than expected performance is due to our unrealistic planning, not to a "shortage" thrust upon us. It is we who need to learn how to manage the energy resources in our world and in our lives.

We can see how calling time a problem or tyrant is a misnomer; it focuses on symptoms rather than on the disease. Time measures the motion and change in activities deter-

> *Time itself does not determine how it is to be used.*

mined by our decisions, motivated by our goals and values. The tyranny of the urgent is more than a question about time. Tension and frustration mount when we are performing the wrong tasks or trying to cram too many of the right activities into a given period.

In order to find the balance we long for, we need to hear the invitation of Jesus: "If the Son sets you free, you will be free indeed" (Jn 8:36). Free to complete the work the Father gives us to do (Jn 17:4).

* * *

Questions for Reflection and Discussion

1. At present do you feel the passage of time to be more a tyrant or a friend?

2. What special events or occasions are you planning?

3. List several occasions when your inner time was very different from outer time. What were the causes?

Scripture Index

Subject Index